# Intermittent Fasting:

# Beginners Guide For Women and Men.

Step-By-Step 30 Day Guide To Get Weight Loss, Build Muscle And Health With Fasting And Diet.

# Table of Contents

# Introduction

As the daughter of a mother who was always dieting, I developed a bad relationship with food, fairly early on in life. I can remember my mother always have special drawers of "diet food" in the kitchen and refrigerator. She would frequently move from one fad to the next. Yes, my mom lost weight, but it never truly seemed to stay off, and this would pave the way for the next yoyo diet to start.

Some of you may be able to relate to this type of tale. Perhaps, a strong role model in your own life unknowingly taught you how to abuse food. Maybe, you're doing it in your own life right now. I get it! There is no judgement.

What I had to decide, after years of being a prisoner to food, was to make a choice. That choice was to set myself free from the clutches of fad diets, yoyo dieting, and fear. Yes, fear. When you are constantly filled with guilt over what you are eating or not eating, this mindset produces fear.

I can recall stressing out about food throughout each one of my three pregnancies. Pregnancy is a time when a woman should enjoy what she eats, focusing on healthy choices, but also letting loose a time or two. I remember feeling guilty about eating cake at my own baby shower.

Something had to change. But, what?

Fast forward about 10 years. My kids are teens and life is not so chaotic anymore. Any mom knows the demands of having babies and toddlers, underfoot. I finally had a chance to do a bit of soul-searching and determine what I wanted to change in my life.

The main struggle I had, and had always had, was food. I decided to research different diets and what I found absolutely fascinated me! I didn't need a diet; I needed a lifestyle change.

When I stumbled upon intermittent fasting (IF) I was perplexed, at first. I thought to myself, "How can anyone do this and not feel famished all day"? There were many other thoughts flying through my mind, as well. I'm sure you are probably having some of the same thoughts that I was.

I am so glad that I put my fear and confusion aside and decided to give IF a try. It's been years since I jumped on the IF train and I couldn't be gladder. This way of eating (WOE) completely changed my life and how I viewed food. I am no longer a slave to what I put in my mouth. I'm free!

Did you know that you can be an intermittent faster and still enjoy holiday dinners and cake on your birthday? Wow, imagine that. You can eat what you like and still lose weight and improve your overall health.

I love it when Thanksgiving comes rolling around because I can enjoy the turkey, stuffing, and pumpkin pie just like everyone else.

In this book, I am going to show you how you can be successful adding IF to your routine. I'll give you a clear idea on why IF works and how to go about getting started. Did you know there are many ways to practice IF? I'll discuss some of them later.

Some of the benefits of IF include weight loss, improved focus, more energy, and better sleep. Who wouldn't want some of those things in their life? You'll want to keep IF as your official WOE for the long haul. Once you get started and see the benefits of scheduled eating, you'll be a believer.

Here's another little tidbit for you....my mother began her IF journey shortly after I did. All those years of fearing food and yoyo dieting came undone after just a month of incorporating fasting into her life. She finally experienced freedom from food. Isn't that wonderful?

You can be free, too. Are you ready to change your life? Are you ready to view food as sustenance and not as an addiction? Are you ready to feel and look better than you ever have before? If so, keep reading. Let's walk this road to food freedom through intermittent fasting, together.

# Chapter 1
# What is Intermittent Fasting (IF)?

So, what is intermittent fasting (IF)? Is it the art of starving oneself? Is it a religious thing? Is it going on a hunger strike? Well, I guess it could be any one of those things, but generally not. To break it down for you, intermittent fasting is a way of life that cycles between periods of fasting and eating. It's truly that simple.

Currently, IF is one of the most popular eating trends in the country, today. However, I don't like to think of IF as a trend, per se. This WOE has been around for a very long time. In fact, our hunter gatherer ancestors used to practice IF every, single day. You may have heard of the Warrior Fast? That's the hunter gatherer way of eating. You hunt all day and eat in the evening.

Other people groups, like Christians, Jews, Muslims, and Buddhists, practice intermittent fasting for religious purposes. The point? They all survived. If you're ever wondering about the safety of IF, just reflect on those who use it regularly as a form of worship or your hunter-gatherer ancestors.

A great aspect about IF is that there are no food restrictions. You can eat what you like. This is what makes following an IF lifestyle so sustainable. Many times, people fall off the diet wagon because they must deprive themselves of the foods they love. Nope. Not the case with intermittent fasting.

Therefore, intermittent fasting isn't necessarily a diet but rather an eating pattern.

Did you know that fasting from time-to-time is far more natural than eating 3 square meals a day with snacks in between? Years ago, people just simply didn't do this. Think about the folks of the

Pioneer days, Men, women, and children where strong and healthy. Most of them only at once or twice a day.

Here are some common myths about intermittent fasting:

## Myth #1 – You Need 3 Meals a Day to be Healthy

This honestly couldn't be further from the truth. I know that most of you have been ingrained to think that 3 meals a day is the way to go. My mother and grandmother and probably all the mothers beyond them have always preached that you need 3 square meals a day in order to survive and be healthy.

I can recall, a child, not liking to eat breakfast, and my mom thought this was just the absolute worst thing that could ever happen.

Please know that western societies are about the only cultures who eat all day long.

There have been plenty of studies to dispel the believe that 3 meals a day is necessary. One study in particular showed that when 1 meal a day is eaten and contains the same number of calories of 3 meals, weight loss is more likely.

## Myth #2 – Breakfast is the Most Important Meal of the Day

As I mentioned above, I never liked eating breakfast and my mom found this to be quite unsettling. However, the claim that breakfast is the most important meal of the day is false. Many people preach that breakfast speeds up metabolism and decreases your desire for food later on in the day. Both of the claims couldn't be further from the truth.

Did you know that these claims about breakfast have been refuted and studied over a 16-week period of a control group of human participants? The results of the subjects showed that their metabolism did not slow down when breakfast was skipped, nor did it show that the subjects binged during lunch and dinner.

Now, please know that it is still possible to intermittent fast and consume breakfast. You just have to make breakfast part of your eating window.

# How is Our Modern Diet a Problem?

Did you realize that the acronym for the Standard American Diet is SAD? It couldn't be more befitting. It *is sad* that our society is pretty much eating itself to death. In today's world, things like obesity, hypertension, heart disease, and diabetes are at an all-time high. If you look at people's weight and health in the 1950's you won't see the issues we see today in such epic proportions.

It all started when we began eating more fast food, adding more sugar to our diets, and consuming low-nutrient meals. These types of "foods" are very addicting. How many times have you eating a jelly doughnut for breakfast and felt famished again within an hour or two?

It's true, you don't have to restrict the foods you eat when you are partaking in IF, however, you do need to be mindful how they are affecting how you feel. You want to be successful at IF and enjoying a variety of healthy foods will help you reach your goals.

One of the biggest problems in American society is how we eat. We eat when we are sad, happy, celebrating, bored, etc. We mindlessly eat while we watch TV, talk on the phone, and work. How many times have you brought a bag of potato chips to the couch and ate the entire bag without even paying attention? Don't feel ashamed, I've done it, too!

We consume foods with tons of carbohydrates, trans fats, and hydrogenated oils. We eat sugar like it's going out of style (I sure wish that it would!). We do all of these things in mass quantity.

The SAD tells us to eat all day long. It also tells us that processed, and carb-laden foods should make up 75% of our diets. Folks, this is a lie. All you have to do is look around you and see that the SAD doesn't work. For me, all I had to do was look in the mirror.

We do not need to be feeding our faces all the time. Every time we feel a little grumble in the stomach we make a mad dash to the dinner table. It's time to undo these unhealthy practices and reclaim our freedom from food.

You may be wondering why some health professionals do not recommend fasting if our SAD diets are so bad. Well, the answer is simple. When we fast, we are not eating a bunch of unhealthy foods. When we don't eat unhealthy foods, things like the fast food industry and processed food companies don't get paid. When we fast, we become healthier, so Big Pharma and doctors don't get a paycheck. Healthy people don't make the healthcare industry any money.

Now, I'm not trying to say that all doctors have an agenda to keep us sick. That would be a false statement and I'm not into lying to people. However, there are some kooky folks out there and it is up to you to determine whether your health care professional has your best interest at heart or is simply wanting to line his or her pockets.

# History of Intermittent Fasting

So, as I mentioned before, intermittent fasting is not a new concept, by any means. Our hunter-gatherer ancestor set the ball in motion for us. However, the idea was thrown into modern society by people like BBC broadcast journalist Dr. Michael Mosley and Dr. Jason Fung.

Dr. Mosley produced a documentary called *Eat Fast, Live Longer* and wrote a book, *The Fast Diet*. Journalist, Kate Harrison, followed right behind Dr. Mosely when she wrote her book, *The 5:2 Diet*. Dr. Jason Fung came out with a 2016 best seller, *The Obesity Code*. These three things helped to generate a positive buzz around IF as people started trying it and reported positive results.

Others have spoken out about the benefits of IF and its effectiveness. Today, there are support groups, social media pages, and all sorts of materials that have been produced about this WOE. People have really latched on to the concept of IF, and their lives are changing because of it.

There are many people who fast for spiritual reasons, too. Fasting has been used by several major religions for thousands of years. For example, people of the Catholic faith fast or abstain from any form of meat during Ash Wednesday, Good Friday, and every Friday during the Lent season. People of the Jewish faith fast for 7 days over the course of the year, especially during Yom Kippur. If you are of the Muslim religion, you won't be consuming any food during the Ramadan season, which lasts a month, from sunup to sundown. Jesus, Himself, was known to fast and did so for 40 days, as foretold in the Bible. There are other eastern religions such as Buddhism and Hinduism that employ fasting quite often as a way to purify the body and increase focus and a sense of mindfulness.

Fasting is actually one of the most ancient and nationally and internationally used traditions in the entire world. Did you know that Hippocrates of Cos (c 460 – c370 BC) is considered, by many modern-day health professionals, to be the father of medicine? This amazing genius of a man had many remedies and therapies for illnesses, including fasting. Hippocrates also believed in prescribing apple cider vinegar, a widely used supplement by the fasting community.

---

*Hippocrates wrote, "To eat when you are sick, is to feed your illness". The ancient Greek writer and historian Plutarch (cAD46 – c AD 120) also echoed these sentiments. He wrote, "Instead of using medicine, better fast today". Ancient Greek thinkers Plato and his student Aristotle were also staunch supporters of fasting.*

---

Source: https://idmprogram.com/fasting-a-history-part-i/

Ancient Greek societies believed that medical treatment could be learned from watching nature. How many times have you caught yourself not eating when you are sick? Think about it. What do humans most often due when they are feeling under the weather? They sleep. The last thing anyone feels like doing when they are ill is consuming a large meal. Animals are the same way. Did you know, that for this reason, fasting has been referred to as the "physician within"? Fasting is a natural instinct that kicks in when both animals and humans are sick. It is a natural form of anorexia, if you will.

> *"Everyone has a physician inside him or her; we just have to help it in its work. The natural healing force within each one of us is the greatest force in getting well. Our food should be our medicine. Our medicine should be our food. But to eat when you are sick is to feed your sickness."*
>
> *- Hippocrates*

Fasting is a practice that has been ingrained into our DNA. It is as old as humans, themselves.

Another thing that the ancient Greeks believed was that fasting helps improved focus, mental clarity, and concentration. You can test this theory by eating a large meal. Do you feel like doing math problems after Christmas dinner? Probably not. You probably feel like crawling onto your recliner and taking a nap. You certainly won't fit the profile of mental alertness.

> *"Instead of using medicine, rather, fast a day."*
>
> *- Plutarch*

Have you ever heard the term, 'food coma"? There is some truth to this funny little saying! When we eat a huge meal, blood stopped up in your digestive tract in order to handle the large influx of food. These leaves less blood flow to the brain. In turn, you feel groggy and fatigued.

There are plenty of other followers of fasting like Philip Paracelsus, who is the founder father of toxicology. He viewed fasting as a remedy. Ben franklin was also known for his knowledge about fasting. Mr. Franklin wrote that the best medicine is not eating and resting.

# Science and Benefits Behind Intermittent Fasting

According to neuroscientist Mark Mattson, cutting your food intake by utilizing fasting a few days a week might help your brain fight off diseases like Alzheimer's and Parkinson's while improving your focus, memory, and emotional status. Mattson's studies have been built on years of research. He has proven there is a direct link between caloric intake and how the brain works. (1)

"Fasting is a challenge to your brain, and we think that your brain reacts by activating adaptive stress responses that help it cope with disease," says Mattson. "From an evolutionary perspective, it makes sense your brain should be functioning well when you haven't been able to obtain food for a while."

When we don't eat for a while, a few things take place within your body. Let's check them out:

- Insulin levels change: The levels of insulin in your blood drop and this helps your body to burn fat (2).
- Human Growth Hormone (HGH) is impacted: When you fast, the levels of HGH in your blood may increase. When this happens, fat burning and muscle gain or facilitated (3).
- Your Cells Begin to Heal: During fasting, your body will initiate the cellular repair process and remove waste products from cells (4).
- Gene expression: Genes and molecules that are linked to longevity and protection against disease begin to change for the better (5).

Studies have found that many of the benefits of IF are directly related to the changes in hormones, gene expression, and how the cells respond to the fasting process.

### What happens when we are continuously eating?

If we are eating 3 squares meals a day plus snacks or 5 to 6 small meals a day, we are doing ourselves more harm than good.

Did you know that when we eat, we are literally ingesting fuel? When we consume fuel (food) we are causing the hormone insulin to rise. Carbohydrates cause insulin to spike quicker and higher than any other fuel source. Protein has a minimal impact on insulin levels and healthy fat has next to zero. The problem is, protein and fats are almost always consumed with carbs. This is a recipe for disaster.

We know that the more insulin is spiked the more inflammatory the body becomes. Carbohydrates essentially turn to glucose in the blood stream, so the body has to burn this form of energy off right away as sugar levels that become too high can be deadly. The increase of insulin is swift and high.

Insulin within your body will direct glucose in your cells to be used as fuel. Then, proteins are broken down into amino acids and extra amino acids are turned into glucose. Please note that protein does not necessarily raise blood glucose, but it will definitely stimulate an insulin response. As stated before, fats have a very low effect on the body's insulin response.

Did you know that insulin stores away excess energy for late ruse? Yep! Insulin has this little annoying thing that it does by converting excess glucose into glycogen and stockpiles it up in the liver. Granted, this needs to happen, so we don't die when consuming sugar, however, we can avoid all of this by fasting.

Now, get this, the liver can only handle so much glucose, right? So, once it reaches maximum capacity, the liver goes and turns the excess glucose into fat. This is how we develop fatty liver syndrome and it is also how we develop visceral fat otherwise known as belly fat.

Yikes!

So, all of this is to say, that if we remain in a fed state, our insulin levels will stay spiked. When our insulin levels stay elevated, we tax our livers and cause weigh gain and fat deposits to occur.

## What Happens When We Engage in Intermittent Fasting?

When we fast, the process you just read about above comes to a screeching halt, turns itself around, and backtracks. Your insulin levels begin to drop. When this happens, your body starts to burn its stored energy for fuel. The first thing to go is all of that glycogen that has been hanging out in your liver. Once that is taken care of, your body begins to convert stored body fat for energy. Say goodbye to those love handles and belly rolls!

Your pretty much exists in two states: fed with high insulin and fasting with low insulin.

You can either store food for energy or burn food as your fuel source. When you balance eating and fasting you will not gain weight. If you spend most of your life eating and storing fuel, you are probably going to end up being overweight.

## Calorie Restriction Vs. Intermittent Fasting

If you are trying to lose weight or are dealing with type 2 diabetes, your doctor or nutritionist has probably recommended that you go on a constant calorie-restricting diet. Did you know that the American Diabetes Association recommends a 500-750 kcal/day energy deficit? They also want you to combine this eating pattern with regular exercise. This approach is usually combined with eating 4 to 6 micro-meals a day.

Although, you may see results in the beginning, this constant calorie-restriction way of living rarely ever works in the long-term.

There was a study conducted with a 9-year follow-up in the UK on over 179,000 overweight people that showed only 3,500 of them got to a healthy weight by the end of the experiment. That's a pretty high failure rate of about 98%.

When you intermittent fast, you are not in a constant state of restricting calories. This is a good thing! How many times have you used portion control and/or calorie restriction as a means to lose weight and found yourself always feeling hungry and lusting over the foods you can't have? Plus, doing this lowers your body's metabolism.

When you burn less calories per day, you'll find that losing weight become harder and gaining weight becomes easier. If you have managed to lose weight, you'll probably put it back on after calorie restriction has subsided. Intermittent fasting doesn't cause any of these things to occur.

# Physical Benefits of IF

### Weight Loss and Belly Fat

Did you know that IF can help you lose fat around your midsection? It sure can! Why is this important? Well, for starters, most people doing IF are doing it to lose weight and to look better. Having a smaller tummy is part of the process.

Losing weight through intermittent fasting is one of the most effective ways to lose weight. If you have extra pounds that you want to get rid of, IF might just be the answer to your prayers. The first thing you need to realize about IF and weight loss/belly fat loss is that it isn't a diet, per se. As you've probably already noticed, diets do not work, at least in the long term, for weight loss. When you engage in a structured way of eating and change your lifestyle, you keep the weight and belly fat off for good. IF can help you maintain your changes for the long haul.

When we lose belly fat, our health begins to improve, significantly. Having a large belly is a sign of metabolic syndrome, which is a condition that creates insulin resistance. Having too much fat around your waist can also make you more susceptible to heart disease.

Losing belly fat is a sign of weight loss. According to a 2014 review of scientific works, IF can encourage weight loss of up to 3-8% over the course of a 3 to 24 weeks period (6). The subjects in the review also lost 4-7% of their waist circumference, which is a sign that they were losing pure belly fat.

Basically, IF helps you to consume fewer calories which boosts your metabolism. This helps you to lose stubborn belly fat and weight.

**Type 2 Diabetes**

Type 2 diabetes is an ailment where there far more glucose in the body than can be handled. Your cells can no longer respond to insulin, causing you to become insulin resistant. This is when you'll need to give yourself insulin injections or take medication. Your liver will become overloaded with fat and will cause you to gain weight when it tries to clean out the excess glucose stores. This is just an all-around bad situation.

Don't worry, there's hope! All you have to do is stop putting sugar into your body. This means stop consuming so many carbohydrates. Then, burn the sugar that remains in your body, off. You can do this by fasting.

Intermittent fasting has been shown to reduce insulin resistance and lowers the risk of type 2 diabetes development. In recent years, type 2 diabetes has become increasingly common. This is due to more and more people being overweight.

When a person is in a state of constant high blood sugar levels, insulin resistance can develop. When you fast, your blood sugar levels decrease. In turn, your chances of developing type 2 diabetes also, decrease.

There was a human study performed on people who were intermittent fasting. The study showed that the fasting blood sugars of the participants had been reduced by 3-6% and the fasting insulin levels had been reduced by 20-31% (7).

When people are dealing with type 2 diabetes, they may wish to consider combing intermittent fasting and a ketogenic diet together. So, during your refeeds, you'll be eating a very low carb and very high healthy fat diet. There are numerous studies to show that this method works in a significant way to reverse type 2 diabetes.

Type 2 diabetes is the only diabetes that is brought on by obesity and/or eating too much sugar. This illness can be reversed through diet and fasting. There are numerous success stories to prove this occurrence. Type 1 diabetes is a whole different story and is something that you are basically born with.

If you have type 1 diabetes, I implore you to speak with your doctor before fasting. You are dealing with a whole different set of issues and fasting can make them worse. Your doctor will more than likely say no to intermittent fasting or the ketogenic lifestyle.

**Oxidative Stress**

Other studies have shown that IF helps reverse the aging process. Say what? Yes! When we fast, we reduce oxidative stress and inflammation from occurring within the body. Each of these things contributes to aging. Oxidative stress has also been linked to many chronic disease (8). There have been several studies conducted to show that IF may encourage the body to resist oxidative stress (9).

**Heart Health**

Here is one of my favorite benefits of IF: It's beneficial for heart health! I like this aspect a lot because of the high incidence of heart problems in my family. I am already predisposed to having them, so this was more reason for me to begin my IF journey.

So, basically, IF helps to improve many risk factors for heart disease such as lowering blood pressure, lower LDL cholesterol and blood triglycerides, improving inflammatory markers and blood sugar levels (9).

Did you know that overtime, high blood sugar from having type 2 diabetes can severely damage the blood vessels and nerves that help your heart to work? The longer you are suffering from diabetes, the greater the chance that you'll develop heart disease. That's scary! There's hope, though. Work at lowering your blood glucose through intermittent fasting, and your risk for heart disease and stroke will significantly reduce.

In addition, intermittent fasting has been shown to lower high blood pressure. Hypertension, high total and LDL cholesterol, high blood triglycerides, and inflammatory markers are all linked with chronic ailments. You can lower the risk of developing all of these things through intermittent fasting.

There have been plenty of studies to prove that intermittent fasting helps lower bad cholesterol and insulin levels, and this will help break up body fat and give you a massive boost in energy. All of these things working together helps the body not to become resistant to insulin, which helps ward of the incidence of succumbing to type 2 diabetes.

Another interesting thing about intermittent fasting and heart health is that it is shown to relieve stress. When we endure constant high levels of stress, we put ourselves at risk of heart attack and stroke. Just fasting for a few days per week can significantly reduce our risk of stress-induced heart disease.

**Induces Multiple Cellular Repair Processes**

Did you know that when you fast your body will initiate waste removal? Yep! It's like your body decides to take out the garbage. When we are in a constant state of digestion, or bodies cannot do this. This process is called autophagy.

During autophagy, your cells break down and metabolize proteins that are of no use to your body. Without autophagy, these proteins build up inside of your cells over the course of time.

When you increase the occurrence of autophagy through IF, you are helping your body to protect itself from various diseases like cancer and Alzheimer's (10).

**Cancer Prevention**

Like we discussed above, fasting increases the incidence of autophagy. Autophagy helps control the growth of cells. Because fasting has beneficial effects on the metabolism, it may lead to a reduction in the risk of cancer.

There haven't been any human studies performed in this theory yet, but there have been a lot of animal studies with very promising results (11).

Although no official studies have been performed, there has been evidence of fasting reducing various chemotherapy side effects in patients suffering from cancer (12).

**Increase in Life Expectancy**

This may come as a shock to you, but IF can actually help you to live longer. There have been studies in rats to back this claim up (13).

Now, granted, even though this theory is far from being proven in people, intermittent fasting has become quite trendy among folks looking to slow down the aging process.

## Autophagy

Experiencing autophagy through intermittent fasting is one of the best benefits of engaging in an IF lifestyle. As you can see from the excerpt above. Autophagy produces some miraculous things to occur within your body. Have you ever wondered how some people, no matter their ages, look so young? If they fast, it is most definitely due to autophagy.

This is why people who fast are said to have found the "Fountain of Youth" because autophagy helps you to look and feel younger. Why wouldn't it? It literally helps your cells repair themselves down to the DNA level.

## Fitness

Intermittent fasting can significantly help you to look fitter. I know, we've heard it a million times that pre and post workout meals are a must. This is true for some people such as those who are intensely training and body builders. However, the rest of us won't be losing any muscle if we fast during our workouts.

Now, if you are keto-adapted, you certainly won't be losing any muscle from fasting, even if you are an athlete.

Fasting helps you to have higher metabolic adaptation that encourage higher training performance and an increase in how well your workouts go in the long run if you consistently exercise in a fasted state.

Do you want improved muscle synthesis? Start working out in a fasted state. You'll notice a marked increase in muscle gains.

Studies have shown that there is a quite a speedy absorption of nutrients after a fasted workout and can improve your response to post workout meals.

There have been numerous fasting studies while people are athletically training. One in particular focused on Muslim athletes during the season of Ramadan. The study found that there was no ill effect on the athletes' performances while in a fasted state.

Another area of fitness that I want to address is muscle mass retention. Intermittent fasting will not cause you to lose muscle mass. Did you know that popular calorie-restricting diets cause a lot more muscle mass depletion than any fasting regimen? In 2010, some researchers observed a panel of patients who engaged in 70 days of alternate day fasting. This means the subjects ate one day and fasted the next.

The muscles of these subjects started off at 52.0 kg and ended at 51.9 kg. As you can see, there was not any loss of muscle mass. However, what these folks did lose was 11.4% body fat. They also saw marked improvements in LDL cholesterol levels and a decrease in triglycerides.

When you fast, your body naturally produces more human growth hormone, and this helps it to keep lean muscle mass and bones in good working order. You don't have to worry about your body cannibalizing its muscles until your overall body fat drops below 4%. This means that most folks aren't at risk of losing their muscles when engaged in an intermittent fasting lifestyle.

# Mental Benefits of IF

### Brain Health

The adage goes, "What's good for the body is good for the brain". I couldn't agree more in terms of intermittent fasting.

Did you know that IF improves all sorts of metabolic occurrences that are known to support brain health? So, basically, you become a genius when you engage in IF. Okay, maybe that isn't completely true, but IF does help promote better focus, clarity, and thought patterns.

Fasting is known to increase the levels of a brain-derived hormone called neurotrophic factor (BDNF) (14). When our brains are lacking in this hormone, studies have shown a link in the increase of depression and other mental health issues (15).

In animal studies, calorie restriction has shown to protect the brain from damages incurred from strokes (16). A study that was performed on mice was shown to demonstrate many neurologic benefits such as having a better attention span, focus, and reaction time. The mice even showed to have a better memory, cognition, and generation of new brain cells! These studies also showed that intermittent fasting reduces inflammation within the brain.

### May Prevent Alzheimer's Disease

There have been a series of case reports that have shown daily short-term fasts to radically improve the symptoms of Alzheimer's Disease symptoms in 9 out of 10 suffers (17). When inflammation is reduces in the brain, the likelihood of developing Alzheimer's Disease is reduced.

Other neurodegenerative diseases have shown to be responsive to fasting such as Parkinson's and Huntington's disease (18).

### Other Benefits...

One of the best things about intermittent fasting in comparison to other diets (IF isn't a diet so there's that) is the fact that you do not need to count calories. Almost all approaches to weight loss involve calorie counting. I don't know about you, but I can't stand counting calories. I've failed other weight loss programs due to this fact, alone.

Anyone can calorie count in the short-term, but it is pretty much impossible over the long-term. You grow weary of constant calorie counting. Nobody wants to be on a diet for the rest of their lives. This is why an intermittent fasting lifestyle works and conventional diets do not.

Another benefit of intermittent fasting is that you don't ever have to go hungry. Think about it, when you are consuming all of your daily caloric needs in an eating window of a few hours, it becomes much harder to binge eat when taking the traditional approach of eating throughout the day. When you fast, you aren't worrying about whether the foods you are eating are good or bad. Fasting is so very simple. You fast when you aren't eating, and you break your fast when you reach your refeed window.

I love the fact that when fasting my body doesn't hang on to its fat stores for dear life. Intermittent fasting is not restrictive like other dieting approaches. When you refeed, you eat until satisfaction and your body responds by continuing to get rid of its fat stores.

Did you know that intermittent fasting is far less demanding than conventional diets? On traditional diets, you can't enjoy things like pizza and French fries. Intermittent fasting doesn't tell you that you can't have these foods during your eating window. Granted, you should eat pizza at every refeed meal, but there is no reason why you can't have it every now and then. Just make sure to slap some veggies on your plate, too. It's all about balance.

Many folks find it beneficial to have some leeway in their food choices. If you are constantly being told that you cannot have cake, you're going to lose it one day and devour an entire cake. Intermittent fasting never deprives you. You'll be less likely to binge on junk food when following an IF schedule.

Lastly, an intermittent fasting lifestyle adapts to you. Isn't that wonderful? So many times, we have to adapt to our diet and that becomes cumbersome. You do not have to stress over the perfect number of MACROS. You don't have to count calories, fat, carbs, and protein. You just don't eat until you do. It's that simple. You have a lot of wiggle room when it comes to IF. Some people fast for 16 hours every day while other only eat 1 meal a day. The sky is the limit when it comes to intermittent fasting.

Intermittent fasting is a lifestyle and not a diet. It is meant to be sustainable for a lifetime.

Whether you are young or old, intermittent fasting can be beneficial for you. This list of benefits is just the tip of the iceberg on how intermittent fasting can make your life better. You may have health issues that aren't even discussed in this book that will begin to improve after starting IF.

A great place to read testimonials about intermittent fasting is Facebook, YouTube, and other social media platform. There are plenty of groups that are loaded with people just like you. Seeking out fasting buddies can be a good thing, too.

# The Stages of Fasting

If you are planning to fast for more than several days at a time, you need to be aware of the three different stages of the process.

## The Cleansing Crisis

In this stage, your body is going to react to the fast. It's kind of like your body saying, "Hey! What's up with this new thing you are doing to me"? You won't be using food for fuel, like you normally do, so naturally, your body is going to react. In response, your body will start using its own resources for energy and expelling a large number of toxins in the process. Your blood, digestive, and renal systems will be working hard to get rid of all the waste products that have accumulated in your system.

Now, this stage of the game can produce some nasty side effects that may make you question why you decided to fast in the first place. Please, don't give up and know that this is a natural part of the process.

Even though you might feel as if you are sick, know that these symptoms are a sure-fire sign that your body is doing exactly what it is supposed to and that the fasting is working.

A lot of people give up on fasting during this stage because they go into the process thinking that they will immediately feel great. Remember, you didn't develop your weight and health problems overnight. It is going to take time to cleanse your body of years of bad eating habits. I won't lie to you, this first stage can be pretty intense depending on your level of toxicity.

## The Fasting Peak

Once your body moves out of the detox stage, it will gradually transition into the fasting peak phase. This is the time when your body starts to calm down and adjust to not getting food every couple of hours. You'll notice that your detox symptoms will start to decrease.

One of the greatest things about this stage of fasting is that you'll start to see marked improvements in your health. Your senses will be heightened, and your mind will feel clearer and sharper. You may even feel rejuvenated and younger.

You'll undoubtedly have more energy as your brain starts to use ketones for fuel instead of glucose. What are ketones? Ketones are created when we don't consume large amounts of carbohydrates. Burning ketones for fuel is essentially burning fat. You want this to happen as it is vital for weight loss.

## The Normal Fasting State

This is the final stage of fasting and is the stage you want to stay in. You'll see your energy levels balance out, even after you've been fasting for some time. Depending on your body, you may see your high energy levels stay the same or drop. Refeeding on a diet low in carbohydrates can encourage energy levels to stay heightened.

### Did you know...

If you are like most people, you probably sleep for a good 6 to 8 hours per night (or day if you're a third shift worker). If you don't, you need to address the reason why you aren't sleeping. Intermittent fasting has been known to help battle problems with insomnia.

Anyway, when you sleep, your body is in a fasted state. When your body is fasting from food, it naturally produces more insulin. When you have an increase in insulin you have increased insulin sensitivity. What does this mean? Quite simply, it means you will lose more fat. This is why intermittent fasting is so amazing. When you spend more time in a fasted state you will literally be melting the pounds away.

Even just skipping breakfast can plunge you deeply into fat loss, or at least get you started.

So many folks are on special diets that require them to eat all kinds of "fat-burning" foods. I have to disagree with these approaches because the only way to truly burn fat is by using fat as a source of fuel. You can't do this unless you are in a state of ketosis.

How do you get into ketosis, quickly? By not eating.

I know some of you are on the ketogenic diet train. I was once on it myself, too. There is nothing wrong with utilizing the keto lifestyle and implementing it with fasting can produce some amazing results. However, not fasting and using keto can hinder your fat loss.

When you fast, your body produces more growth hormone. This is the hormone you produce when you are in a state of weight loss. When involved in an intermittent fasting program, your levels of growth hormone usually increase. It is when your levels of growth hormone peak that you will lose the most weight.

**Some Things to Consider...**

1. Intermittent fasting may sound like a high-tech term taken straight out of a medical journal, but it is really quite simple. All it means is you are going to spend periods of planned time without eating.
2. Did you know that everyone practices intermittent fasting every night? Yep! When you are asleep, you are intermittently fasting.
3. There is a lot of research left to be conducted on the benefits of IF, however, studies have shown that this way of eating significantly improves blood pressure health, can potentially reduce the risk of cancer, helps to control blood sugars, and so much more.
4. There are many different methods to intermittent fasting. We will cover a handful of them in this book. You are not limited to how your approach the IF lifestyle. One of the great things about IF is that you can customize it to fit your needs.
5. Intermittent fasting is pretty much safe for everyone who is healthy, well-nourished, and 18 and over. However, there are some folks who simply cannot and should not do

it. Make sure you have a good understanding of what healthy weight loss is and the fundamentals of nutrition.

# Benefits of IF in the Long Term

All of the mental and physical benefits of fasting that we spoke about earlier have long-term lasting effects. If you keep up with a consistent fasting routine, you'll continue to reap the benefits.

We've covered how intermittent fasting helps keep insulin levels under control by reducing insulin resistance. This can only lead to good things in your future. For one, in totally decreases your risk of type 2 diabetes.

Did you know that by decreasing insulin resistance you are increasing your body's ability to transport glucose more efficiently to your cells through your bloodstream? Just another bonus of IF.

You already know that intermittent fasting helps fight inflammation. Over the long term, keeping inflammation at bay within your body decreases the symptoms of chronic inflammatory diseases. If you don't have these issues to begin with, chances are, you probably won't develop them if you are consistent with fasting.

Intermittent fasting helps controls blood pressure, triglyceride levels, and bad LDL cholesterol. Keeping these numbers good will help protect your heart, over time. Isn't it amazing that fasting can help your heart stay healthy and strong?

Another major long-term benefit that IF brings is the effects of sustained weight loss. If you follow an intermittent fasting lifestyle, your weight is going to be at a healthy number. This means that all of the health problems associated with obesity will no longer be a card dealer in your life. You'll spend your life looking and feeling great.

If you are prone to sickness, you'll see that intermittent fasting will help better your immune response by creating a stronger immune system. Did you know that your body stores toxins in your fat cells? So, when these fat cells are used as an energy source, those toxins get expelled. When you fast, your body is forced to conserve energy in whatever ways possible. One of the most common ways that your body does this is by getting rid of immune cells that are necessarily needed. This includes damaged and compromised cells, too. This process forces your immune system to function at a higher level. Think about it, during fasting your body is getting rid of dysfunctional immune cells and replacing them with healthy, strong ones.

Did you know that science has shown this process to be beneficial for patients who are undergoing chemotherapy? Yep! Studies have shown that patients who fasted three days before a chemo treated avoided a ton of the immune system damages that chemo sometimes causes.

Another benefit of intermittent fasting is that your hunger levels will decrease. Yes, in the beginning, you'll feel like you are starving, but this side effect will go away overtime and will stay away.

Normally, people feel the pangs of hunger within about 4 hours of having their last meal. That's crazy! However, through consistent intermittent fasting, your body is going to adapt to not being fed all of the time. This means, the incidence of hunger is going to decrease.

You don't have to worry that fasting will make you so hungry that you'll binge eat. Studies have shown that after a 24-hour fast, caloric intake does increase by 20%. However, with consistent fasting, this increase disappears because your hunger levels go down and your appetite dwindles.

Many times, hunger comes in waves like the ocean. If you choose to simply ignore the hunger, it will eventually go away. However, if the feeling gets to strong for you, simply drink tea, coffee, and water.

Another thing to keep in mind when fasting is your blood sugar levels. So many people worry that their blood sugar will crash when fasting. Nobody wants to feel shaky and sweaty due to low blood sugar. This just doesn't happen during fasting. Your body needs glucose in order for your blood sugar to bottom out. You aren't eating during your fast, so you don't have any glucose to use up. Think about it, while you sleep, you are essentially fasting, right? You don't have a blood sugar crash in the middle of the night, do you? Of course not.

Now, there are exceptions such as people who are diabetic and those who are taking certain medications. Please speak with your doctor before beginning any type of fast.

## Possible Side Effects of IF

You should always consult your health care professional before starting any weight loss regime or changing up the way you eat. Intermittent fasting isn't for everyone. Some folks can experience more side effects than others. Let's talk about some of the more common ones, first.

So, the most complained about side effect of IF is hunger. Yes, you are going to be hungry when you first begin a fasting regime. It's just going to happen so plan on it. Think about it, you can't go from eating 3 meals a day plus snacks to hours without food and not feeling a few rumbles in your tummy.

Your body needs time to adjust to your new WOE. Trust the process. You won't feel famished forever, I promise you. You just have to ignore those hunger pangs as best as you can. You'll want to drink plenty of water because often times, dehydration makes us feel like we are starving half to death.

In addition to hunger pangs, you may feel weak. Don't be alarmed by this. No, you aren't starving, however, your body is adjusting to not being fed all the time. Feeling weak is a temporary side effect and will go away as your body adjusts.

Brain fog is another reported side effect that many people feel when they first start fasting. However, some folks claim that their mental focus is crisper than it has ever been in their lives when they begin IF. So, basically, it depends on the person.

Again, and I cannot stress this enough, consult your doctor before you begin a fasting program. This is especially true for people who have pre-existing medical conditions. These conditions include, but are not limited to:

- Diabetes
- Problems with blood sugar regulation
- Hypotension
- On medications
- Underweight
- Have an ongoing or a history of eating disorder
- Women who are trying to get pregnant
- Women who are pregnant
- Women who have a history of absent menstrual periods
- Women who are nursing an infant

Please bear in mind, that although IF isn't for everyone, it does have an excellent safety profile. There isn't anything hazardous about abstaining from food a little while longer than you normally do if you are a healthy adult.

# How Long Can You last Without Food?

Fasting isn't easy, especially when you are first starting out. In the beginning stages, you may feel ravenously hungry. This intense level of hunger may lead you to believe that you are starving to death. I assure you, you are not. Your mind may be filled with images of your muscles breaking down and all sorts of horrible things happening. Don't give in to these thoughts.

Did you know that Mahatma Gandhi fasted for 21 days straight and only took in small swallows of water? Throughout history, we are told people without food and water survived for 10 to 14 days at a time. These incidences are extreme cases. What you are doing, is not.

There have been many studies performed on subjects who were engaged in hunger strikes as well as religious fasts. Each study proved that humans have the capacity to survive without food for much longer than Gandhi did during his 21 day fast.

There is a story of a monk who set out to fast for 40 days in a row. He was under medical supervision, so his case was well-documented. After 36 days into the fast, the monk's doctors stepped in because he was significantly weak and experienced low pressure when he stood up. The monk ended up fasting 15 days longer than Gandhi!

Another study followed 33 prisoners of war who decided to go on a hunger strike. Each of these prisoners fasted between 6 and 24 days before having to be hospitalized for dehydration. Their fast was recorded as being "uncomplicated".

I share these studies with you to ease your mind. You will not die from intermittent fasting and your muscles will not start to cannibalize on themselves. When you start feeling so hungry that you could eat an entire cow, keep in mind that this feeling is normal, and it will decrease as you continue on your IF journey.

As always, pay attention to the signals that your body is giving you. You'll know when you should end a fast.

**Refeeding Syndrome and Intermittent Fasting**

I want you to be aware of some of the health issues that can arise from engaging in extended fasts. An extended fast is not eating anything at all for more than 5 days. One of these issues is called refeeding syndrome. Typically, people who intermittent fast do not have to worry about this problem because they don't generally fast that long. In fact, fasting for more than 24-hours at a time is generally not recommended.

Refeeding syndrome is caused by potentially fatal shifts in the balance of electrolytes in the body after eating directly following a period of undernourishment. Again, this isn't something that you need to worry about unless you are not consuming calories for more than 5 days.

# CHAPTER 2
# Getting Started

In this chapter, we are going to discuss the various methods of intermittent fasting and how to accomplish them. Currently, there are 7 popular methods of IF. We will go into the basics of each one. You'll be able to get a clear picture of which method will work best for you. You may even choose to do a combination of some of them.

I'll also cover which types of fasting is best for general health, weight loss, muscle gain, and for women.

Lastly, I'll end this chapter with a complete 30-day guide of a combination of all 7 types of fasting methods. It'll help your first month of fasting go smoother. Plus, you can try out all 7 variations to see which ones work best for you.

# 7 Popular IF Methods

### Eat-Stop-Eat

This style of intermittent fasting was designed by weight-loss superstar, Brad Pilon. This type of IF is based on when you eat rather than what you eat. Pilon says he has scientific evidence that indicates short, regular fasts promote weight loss and better muscle retention than traditional diets that eliminate certain food groups. This type of fasting requires you to fast up to twice a week and it doesn't require you to give up your favorite foods.

The basics of East-Stop-Eat are:

- Fast once or twice per week
- Aim for 24-hours of caloric restriction at a time during your fast
- During eating days, women should consume 2,000 calories and men should consume 2,500
- Never fast on consecutive days
- Do not exceed more than 2 fasts per week
- Eat whatever foods you want during feed days
- Only consume water (sparkling/plain), coffee, tea, and diet soda on fast days

## 5:2

The 5:2 method of intermittent fasting is currently one of the most popular forms of IF, today. It is also known as "The Fast Diet". However, I don't really like calling it a "diet" because it truly is a lifestyle or WOE. Basically, what you're going to do is eat a regular diet 5 days a week and only consume between 500 – 600 calories the other 2 days. This method was made popular by British journalist, Michael Mosley.

The basics of 5:2 are:

- Eat normally 5 days a week
- Consume between 500 – 600 calories 2 days a week
- Do not overeat/binge on non-fasting days
- Eat and drink whatever you want on fasting days just as long as it doesn't exceed 500-600 calories

## Alternate Day Fasting

Alternate day fasting is the process in which you will eat 25% of your total calories on one day and eat regularly on the next. You keep on repeating this cycle. This type of fasting requires you to calculate your average daily intake of calories on eating days and figure out 25% of those calories for your fasting days.

For example, if you normally eat 1800 calories, you'd consume no more than 450 calories on your fasting day.

The basics of alternate day fasting are:

- Eat a normal amount of food one day
- Consume no more than 25% of your average caloric intake on the next day
- Repeat the process
- There are no restrictions as to what you can and cannot eat

**16:8 Method**

The 16:8 IF method is one of the most popular ways of fasting. It is actually a great beginning step. It involves limiting consuming foods and caloric-beverages to a set window of 8 hours per day. Once your window closes, you abstain from food for 16 hours, straight. You can repeat the cycle as often as you want.

Some folks do the 16:8 method all the time while others only implement it a few times a week.

The basic of 16:8 fasting are:

- Eat any type of food and beverages that you want during an 8-hour window of your choosing
- Abstain from consuming calories for the next 16 hours
- You may drink non-calories containing beverages during your fasting window
- 16:8 fasting can be practiced all week long or just a couple of days per week

**The Warrior Diet**

In 2001, The Warrior Diet was created Ori Hofmekler. Ori was a member of the Israeli Special Forces team. He eventually turned into a fitness and nutrition guru.

The idea of The Warrior Diet is to eat like an ancient warrior. You'll eat very little throughout the day and then feast like a king during the evening. Hofmekler says that "this way of eating is designed to improve the way we eat, feel, perform, and look". The Warrior Diet stresses the body through reduced food intake which encourages survival instincts to kick in.

One of the things Ori Hofmekler wants folks to know is that the Warrior Diet is not strictly science based but rather based on his own belief system.

The basics of The Warrior Diet are:

- Under eat for 20 hours per day
- Eat as much food as you want during the evening
- Consumer small amounts of dairy products, hard boiled eggs, raw fruits and veggies, and non-calorie beverages
- After 20 hours, you can binge on any foods you desire within a four-hour window
- Healthy, unprocessed food choices are encouraged during the re-feed window but not essential

**Spontaneous Meal Skipping**

This is probably the easiest of all the ways to intermittent fast. Spontaneous meal skipping is just that...you skip meals when you feel like it. There is no structure to this form of IF. The best way to follow this type of IF is to skip meals when you aren't feeling all that hungry. There is no reason to eat just because the clock strikes noon or the rooster crows.

The basics of spontaneous meal skipping are:

- Don't eat a meal that you aren't hungry for
- Skip at least 1 to 2 meals per week
- Make sure to eat healthy foods when you do eat

**One Meal A Day (OMAD)**

Eating one meal a day, otherwise known as OMAD, is a very simple way to fast. You don't really have to think about food or plan your meals because you literally are only faced with eating once per day. There are no restrictions on what your one meal needs to be, either.

You get to pick the time of day you want to eat your meal and you do so in a one-hour window. The other 23 hours of the day you spend drinking water, black coffee, and tea.

The basics of OMAD are:

- Fast for 23 hours a day
- Do not consume any calories during fasting
- Choose a 1-hour timeframe in which you'll consume your meal
- Do not eat less than 1200 calories during refeeding
- No-calorie beverages may be consumed during fasting hours (Dr. Jason Fung says bone broth is fine as well as a small amount of cream in your coffee.... this is debatable)
- There are no food restrictions on your OMAD

# Which Type of IF Will Be Best for You?

Honestly, any one of these methods work well for healthy and already well-nourished adults. However, convenience and time are factors that may play into the type of IF you choose to do on a regular basis. A lot of people enjoy combining a few of the different methods together. In time, you'll know which method or methods are right for you.

One place that most beginners like to start at is the 16/8 method. This type of IF is easier to transition into when you're just starting out because you get a bigger eating window. You may be thinking, "16 hours is a long time to fast"! Yes, it can be, however, you're probably going to be spending 8 of those hours sleeping. Yep, sleeping counts towards your fast as you aren't consuming any food.

A lot of people will start there fast at 8 pm and fast until 12 pm, the next day. There eating window is open from noon to 8 pm. If you are just starting out on your intermittent fasting journey, 16:8 might be a good stepping stone for you.

The 5:2 Diet is another great place for beginners to start. It only requires that you fast for 2 days a week and many people find this to be incredibly doable. It leaves plenty of room for going to parties, events, and other types of activities where there will be eating.

The only kicker to this type of fasting is that on your diet days, you can only consume very little calories. It is suggested that women consume 500 and men, 600. Even though you are only doing this twice a week, some people find it difficult and get derailed.

Eat-Stop-Eat is similar to the 5:2 Diet in that you only fast once or twice a week. However, on your fasting days, you eat absolutely nothing. If you are a person who has tried some of the other fasts and want to take a more extreme approach, this method might be a good fit for you.

Alternate Day Fasting is a pretty easy concept, but it falls into the extreme category as the Eat-Stop-Eat IF method. If you don't have self-control issues and aren't totally new to fasting, this method may be right for you.

You also need to be good at figuring out calories and keeping track of them. So, if you don't like math, you may want to skip out on Alternate Day fasting, altogether.

Personally, I like the concept of The Warrior Diet, but it's probably best for people who are athletic and into extreme lifestyles. After all, that's how warriors lived their lives. If you don't mind eating small amounts of raw foods during the day and then feasting at night, you may want to give this form of fasting a shot. If you do lead an active lifestyle, you may find that your energy levels will improve with this method of IF.

If you naturally skip meals, you may want to consider the Spontaneous Meal Skipping method. This is type of fasting is super easy and is great for folks who are busy and don't always have time to eat. If you find yourself not always hungry at mealtimes, you don't have to eat, so fast.

Lastly, One Meal A Day aka OMAD, is one of my favorite ways to fast. It is super easy to do as there are no restrictions other than don't eat for 23 hours. You can have whatever you want in your one-hour eating window. OMAD is a wonderful tool, for those suffering from food addiction, to use. You are only having to think about food once per day. For some, this can be quite a blessing in their health and wellness journey.

# Fasting and Children

It is pretty much agreed upon by all fasting gurus and doctors alike that children should avoid fasting. If your kid happens to skip a meal here and there, don't worry. They'll be fine. However, to actively implement IF into their lives, is not advisable.

Kids don't think like adults. When you start encouraging fasting, your child can get the wrong idea and think that he or she is fat, ugly, and not worthy. This can lead to an eating disorder. For more information, check out Dr. Jason Fung, who elaborates quite a bit on this subject.

Children need more calories than adults for proper development and brain growth. Do not put your child on any diet or fasting regime without seeking medical advice, first.

# How to Start Your Fasting Program

### Fasting for General Health

If you are simply fasting to improve your health, your first step should be to visit your doctor and let him know your plans. You should ask your doctor for a complete physical examination and blood work panel. This will give you and your doctor a baseline of what need to be improved.

Once you get the green light from your doctor to go ahead and start fasting, you can pretty much choose any of the methods we talked about above s all of them will improve your health.

Start slowly, if you have never fasted before and work your way up to the more extreme fasts. Take into consideration your specific health issues. If you are diabetic, a longer fast may not be suitable for you. Again, speak to your doctor about your health concerns, preexisting conditions, and whether intermittent fasting will be a positive impact on them or not.

### Fasting for Weight Loss

Choosing to fast for the sole purpose of losing weight is what 95% of you are reading this book for. Why? Because any and all fasting works to help you shed the pounds. Just as I mentioned above, go see your doctor before starting a fasting regimen, especially if you have a considerable amount of weight to lose.

You'll want a complete physical and bloodwork performed so you and your doctor will know of any health concerns.

Any fasting method is going to help you lose weight. However, some methods work more quickly than others. If you're looking to get a jump on your weight loss, I recommend going with OMAD. This type of fasting takes a bit to get used to, especially if you are accustomed to eating 3 meals a day. However, once you get over the initial hump, you'll be smooth sailing.

OMAD generally produces results rather quickly and this can be encouraging for people. If you are planning to exercise or lead an active lifestyle, The Warrior Diet might be a good plan for you in terms of weight loss.

Which leads me into my next point....

**Fasting for Muscle Gain**

Using The Warrior Diet method for gaining muscle is the best route to go down. I'll assume that you are already exercising or at least plan to be, since you are wanting to gain muscle. Eating small amounts of raw fruits and veggies and dairy during the day can be quite beneficial to retaining muscle. The combination of this and an exercise program can really help you to bulk up.

Because you have been working out during the day, your energy expenditure will be high. You'll enjoy getting to feast during the evening. Get ready to watch your muscles grow!

**Fasting for Women**

If you are a woman looking to start an intermittent fasting routine, there really aren't too many things that you need to be doing different than the men. However, a modified approach may be necessary under certain circumstances.

Are you trying to get pregnant? If so, I wouldn't do any extreme form of fasting. There have been reports of menstrual cycles being a bit out of whack when women fast. You don't want to be causing anything funny to happen with your reproductive health when you're trying to conceive.

Are you already pregnant? If so, put this book down and don't pick it back up until after your baby has been born and you aren't breastfeeding. Fasting just isn't a good idea for a pregnant mom.

During times of refeeding, you won't need as many calories as the guys do. I know, bummer, right? You'll be fine, I promise. The amount is only about a 500-calorie difference.

Other than that, women are free to fast just like the guys.

## Fasting and Meditation

Meditation is a way to clear and clarify your mind and spirit. Many people use fasting as a way to reach a heightened state of mindfulness and they do this in conjunction with meditation. There are many techniques to meditation, all of which you can practice during fasting.

Did you know that in Buddhism, the word "meditation" is equal to a word like "sports"? This is because meditation isn't just one activity but rather an umbrella of different things. Different meditation practices require different skills of the mind.

I've found that practicing meditation while fasting is quite beneficial. When our bodies aren't taking in food and in a state of constant digestion, our minds are clearer and more focused. Normally, one may find it difficult to sit for an extended period of time and literally think about nothing. However, fasting makes this process a lot easier to achieve.

Let's take a look at some of the different ways to meditate.

### Concentration

This form of meditation encourages you to sit and contemplate a single point. You could focus on your fast, if you like. This type of meditative state typically has you take a breath and repeat a single word or mantra, of some sort. You should focus on something like a candle flame or light bulb during this time. Some people listen to the repetitive gong, or count beads on a necklace.

You should try this form of meditation for just a few minutes at a time, especially if you are a beginner. Sitting and focusing on one thing for extended periods of time can be frustrating as we often loose our focus. This defeats the purpose of meditation.

Each time you engage in this form of meditation, your level of concentration will improve.

### Mindfulness

This form of meditation involves observing the thoughts that enter your mind. The point isn't to get overly involved in those thoughts or to be judgmental of them, but rather to be aware of each thought as it enters the mind.

During fasting, thoughts of food, health, and weight loss may freely enter your though system. Focus on each of these areas and explore them, a bit. Mindfulness meditation allows you to see your thoughts and how you feel and respond towards them. The more you practice mindfulness meditation the more you'll be aware of your tendency to quickly judge any experience, whether good or bad, as pleasant or unpleasant. You'll soon develop an inner balance of your thoughts.

### Benefits of Meditation

Meditation allows you to become more relaxed and Intune with your thoughts. As you engage in intermittent fasting, you may find yourself questioning why you are doing this. Your mind might dive beyond weight loss and health issues. This can be a wonderful thing! You'll find that consistent meditation will help you on your fasting journey.

Other benefits include:

- Lowers blood pressure
- Improved circulation
- Lowers heart rate
- Helps you to sweat less
- Slows down breathing
- Creates a feeling of calmness
- Decreases blood cortisol levels
- Heightens feelings of well-being
- Reduces stress
- Plunges you into a deeper relaxed state

These are all short-term effects of meditation. However, they can leave you feeling well and rested the entire day long. When you aren't feeling anxious or worried, your fast is going to go a lot smoother. You'll find yourself feeling more confident and capable.

**Simple Steps for Beginner Meditation**

1. Find a quiet spot to sit or lie down, comfortably. This can be your favorite chair, couch, cushion, or bed. Some people, weather permitting, even enjoy going outside and laying under a tree. Make sure the clothes you are wearing aren't constricting and are comfortable.
2. Close your eyes and relax.
3. Pay attention to your breathing and control it. Breathe in and out, naturally.
4. Focus on your breathing and how your chest rises and falls with each inhale and exhale. If your mind begins to wander, re-center your focus on your breathing.

You can do this for 2 or 3 minutes, to start. As you become better at meditating, you'll be able to do it for longer periods of time.

# Intermittent Fasting and Gut Health

Did you know that 60% of your body's immune response lies within your gut? Studies have been showing that gut health is seriously important for overall health. Fasting can help you improve and maintain your gut health as well as heal a stressed gut.

We often look at all of the health benefits that intermittent fasting gives us, but gut health is sometimes overlooked. Researchers have found that fasting goes beyond brain and body benefits and can enhance the amount of good gut flora that protects us against metabolic syndrome.

This all goes back to eating a healthy diet during your feeding periods. No, you certainly do not have to do this but if you want a healthy gut, I advise that you do. So many people eat unhealthy foods before they go to bed and this does nothing good for their guts. If you plan to refeed late in the evening, try to eat some gut-loving foods like yogurt and kefir with your meal.

To capitalize on all of the benefits of fasting, you must consume a gut-healthy diet. This means, you need to stay away from non-organic foods, GMO-laden foods, and overly processed foods. A diet rich in whole foods will definitely help you achieve your health and wellness goals.

**Strategies for Great Gut Health While fasting**

- Fix your gut problems before you start an IF lifestyle
- Be mindful about food sensitives and avoid those foods

- Add lots of fermented and cultured foods to your feeding window
- Combine IF with a ketogenic diet
- Keep in mind that your gut health is affected by more than just the foods you eat. Try to limit stress, insomnia, and lack of exercise from your life

# 30 Days of Intermittent Fasting

In this helpful 30-day guide, I'll be giving you a day-by-day example of what the various forms of fasting will look like. You can use this guide as a starting point to give all 7 forms of fasting a shot. Over the next month, you'll be able to decide which method or methods work best for you.

I know, that whenever a new diet trend or way of eating hits the airwaves, I want to give it a thorough testing before I fully commit. Hopefully, this 30-day guide can help get you started on your IF journey.

Remember, some of these methods are harder than others and if you must modify them, that's okay. This is your journey. IF is about food freedom.

There really is no right or wrong way to intermittent fast, unless you're eating all day long, every day. Then, yep, you're doing it wrong. I'm sure you won't be doing that, though.

Take each day slowly and remember your goals. Write them down if you need, too. This sometimes helps people to stay focused and on track.

You're doing this to better your health, to look and feel great, and to break the chains of food addiction. You've got this.


## Day 1

Today, is the first day of your IF journey. We are going to start out slowly by doing the 5:2 method. We are going to do this plan for the first 7 days of the month.

Today you will eat as you normally would. Go ahead and enjoy breakfast, lunch, dinner, and a couple of snacks if you would like.

There are no foods or beverages that are off limits.

Keep track of how many calories you consume. Try not to binge eat on more foods and drinks than normal. Remember, this method is NOT about binging on your non-fast days.

Before you begin, weigh and/or measure yourself. Record your findings.

## Day 2

How did you enjoy your first day of "fasting"? I bet you didn't think you'd be eating during it.

Did you keep track of the number of calories you consumed? Great! Now, think about this number. Does it seem way over what you typically eat? Is it way under? You shouldn't be answering "yes" to either of those questions. You need to eat normally during your non-fast days.

Don't sweat it if you went a little crazy. You're just getting started.

On your second day of the 5:2 plan you are going to continue eating normally.

## Day 3

How did you do yesterday? Did you enjoy the foods that you love? Let's check out those calorie numbers, shall we? Are they normal as to what you typically consume? Yes? Great! I'm proud of you.

Okay, so today is the day. Instead of eating normally, you are going to only consume 500 calories if you are a woman and 600 calories if you are a man. Make sure to drink lots of water.

You may choose whatever food and drinks you want, just as long as they don't exceed your calorie goals for the day.

If you are feeling famished, sip on water, black coffee, tea, or any other non-calorie drinks.

## Day 4

How was your first day officially fasting? Granted, this wasn't a "clean fast" because you were able to consume some calories. However, that doesn't mean that it still wasn't challenging. Only eating 500 to 600 calories is tough, especially when you are used to eating a whole lot more.

You'll be happy to know that today is going to be a normal eating day.

There is one little kicker though, I want you to try and focus on healthy foods. Many times, we tend to pig out on processed foods, sugar, and other junk that isn't good for us. Try to make today all about your health.

Record how you feel at the end of the day.

## Day 5

How did it go yesterday? Did you make some healthy choices? I know it isn't easy to give up the foods you love, especially when you are told that there aren't any food restrictions when doing IF.

To reiterate, there are NOT food restrictions during IF, however, you find that your health and weight issues will clear up a lot quicker if you are eating a more balanced diet on your refeed days.

So, what did you record about your day yesterday? How did you feel? Do you find that eating more whole foods leaves you with more energy, less bloating, and helping you to sleep better?

Let's go ahead and do another day of normal eating. You can continue on with healthy food choices or eating whatever you want. It's totally up to you.

## Day 6

Another day of normal eating has passed. You're really trucking along like a champ! I know you may be thinking that you really aren't fasting, but you are! The days of only consuming 500 – 600 calories really do create a deficit in the number of calories you consume in a weekly basis.

Speaking of which, go ahead and make today a 500-600 calorie day.

To make eating a bit easier and stress-free, considering picking up a TV dinner that only contains your allotted number of calories. There are plenty on the market that are healthy choices, too.

You also have the option of splitting your calories in half and eating them at 2 different times during the day.

## Day 7

You made it to day 7! Great work. How did your fast yesterday go? Hopefully, it was a little bit easier than the first one you did at the start of the week. Fasting will gradually get easier the more you do it.

You'll be eating normally today, but with a twist. I want you to add spontaneous meal skipping to the mix. Choose any meal that you want and skip it.

Today, I'd like you to weigh yourself and/or take your measurements to check your progress. Record your findings.

## Day 8

How are you feeling today? Did you enjoy skipping a meal yesterday or was it challenging? If it was challenging, consider skipping a different meal in the future. Sometimes, it's all about timing.

Today, I want you to give the Eat-Stop-Eat method a try. I don't want you to consume any food for 24-hours. So, if your last meal or snack was at 6pm yesterday, you won't eat again until 6pm this evening.

Drink all of the non-caloric beverages that you want. Staying hydrated is key.

Once your 24-fast completes, please consume 2000 calories if you are a woman and 2500 calories if you are a man. Eat whatever want, but keep in mind that healthy choices will lead to quicker results.

### Day 9

How did your very first 24-hour fast go? I bet it was challenging and that is normal. If you sailed through it without any hunger pangs, you're a fasting natural. Whichever the case may be, don't be too hard on yourself.

Today, we are going to jump into The Warrior Diet. You should never do two 24-hour fasts back-to-back as detailed in the Eat Skip Eat guidelines.

So, today I want you to eat very small amounts of raw veggies and fruits, dairy, and hard-boiled eggs. When I say small, I mean one piece of fruit, one veggie, a hard-boiled egg or two, and maybe a few chunks of cheese. You will do this for 20 hours. Make sure to drink as many non-caloric beverages as you want.

Once 20 hours ends, you can feast on whatever foods you want over a 4-hour window. Keep in mind, you are trying to eat like an ancient warrior so the healthier and less processed foods you consume, the better.

## Day 10

Good morning, warrior! How did eating like a hunter/gatherer go? I bet you were excited to feast during your 4-hour window!

Guess what? You get to be a warrior again today by completing another round of this type of IF method.

If you feasted on foods that weren't all that great, yesterday, try to add a few healthier options to your plate today.

## Day 11

I bet you could pass for a Viking, today. How do you feel eating a Warrior's Diet? Make sure you are thinking about the different forms of IF you've tried thus far. Journal about the ones that you like best and why.

Today, I want you to eat normally but toss in another round of spontaneous meal skipping. Perhaps, you can shoot for skipping 2 meals instead of one.

Many people find that skipping breakfast and lunch are the easiest meals to give up. However, this is your journey so skip the meals you feel work best for you.

## Day 12

Which meal or meals did you skip, yesterday? If you skipped 2 meals, how did you feel when it was time to eat? Journal about your findings.

Today, we are going to go down the 16:8 pathway. I think you'll like this IF method, as most people do.

So, if your last meal was at 8pm, yesterday evening, you won't wait again until noon, today. Your eating window will then close at 8pm. Remember, these times are just examples. You can choose any 16-hour fasting window that you want. It is in your best interest to utilize sleeping times to your advantage.

When your 8-hour refeed window opens, feel free to dine on whatever you want. Be mindful not to binge, though. A person can pack in a ton of calories during an 8-hour timespan. You don't want to eat more than you normally would during this timeframe. Consider having 1 large meal and a snack.

Make sure to stay hydrated. You are free to drink any non-calorie beverages during your 16-hour fasting window that you want.

## Day 13

Good morning! I hope your first 16:8 fast went amazingly well. Whether it did or did not, we are doing it again today.

Follow all the same rules as yesterday.

## Day 14

You are certainly a fasting pro by now. I can just feel it! The 16:8 method is probably becoming second nature to you.

You are going to get some more practice today by doing another round of it. Keep going! You can do this. Take a look at those goals you wrote down.

Today is weigh-in and measurement day. Record your progress.

## Day 15

You've made it to the half-way point! Hooray for you! How are you feeling about this whole fasting thing? I bet you are making lots of progress.

If you are growing weary of the 16:8 method, well, today is your lucky day because we are going to switch gears a bit.

Today, I welcome you to OMAD. You'll be fasting for 23 hours straight. So, if your last meal was at 8pm yesterday, you'll be having your one meal a day at 7pm. You only get a one-hour window on this IF method. So, make sure to consume your food within 60-minutes.

Whether you're a man or a woman, your meal should be no less than 1200 calories. You get one plate of food and one calorie-containing beverage.

On this method, going for a second plate of food is frowned upon. Make sure you are drinking only water, tea, and black coffee. I, personally, drink diet soda. However, the creator of the OMAD method says to steer clear of it. Use your own discretion.

## Day 16

How was your OMAD experience? What did you learn about yourself from it? I find OMAD to be my favorite way of fasting because it is so simple.

I want you to give OMAD another go today.

Don't forget to drink plenty of non-calorie beverages.

## Day 17

Hello! Are you feeling a little more pep in your step today? Many folks report that they sleep a lot better when eating one meal a day.

You may even be feeling some symptoms of detox by this stage in the game. Please know that these symptoms are normal. Keep going! However, if you are really feeling poorly, you can always revert back to the 5:2 method.

Let's go for OMAD again, today.

## Day 18

I am so excited for you! You've just completed 3 days of OMAD. That's something to be proud of. I bet you are noticing some serious health and weight benefits, by now. If you aren't don't fret. Sometimes it takes people a little longer before they see results. We are all different.

Today, we are going to step away from OMAD and go for Alternate Day Fasting. I want you to eat normally, today. Just like the Eat-Stop-Eat IF method, you need to pay attention that you don't binge eat, just eat normally.

Pay attention to the amount of calories you typically eat on a non-fasting day. You'll need this info for tomorrow.

## Day 19

Did you remember to think about how many calories you consume on a typical non-fasting day? Great. Today, I want you to only consume 25% of that amount. For example, if you eat 1800 calories on a normal day, you will only eat 450 calories on your fasting day.

There are no restrictions as to what you choose to eat.

Make sure to drink plenty of non-caloric beverages.

## Day 20

How did your day of only consuming 25% of your normal caloric intake go? I bet you breezed right through it. You've lived through some very tough forms of IF. Alternate Day fasting should be a piece of cake...or air...for you.

Let's give it another shot today, shall we?

Eat normally, today. There are no restrictions on the type of foods you can eat. HOWEVER, healthy is always best.

## Day 21

You are 3 weeks in! Go you! Only 9 more days left until you've reached your 30-day IF goal. I'm proud of you.

Let's continue on with Alternate Day fasting today. Only consume 25% of your non-fasting day caloric intake.

Keep yourself hydrated!

Weight and measure yourself. Record your progress.

## Day 22

You are really doing well and deserve a pat on the back for all your hard work.

Let's go back to basics and hop on the 5:2 train again, shall we?

Eat a normal, well-balanced diet today.

## Day 23

How are you doing today? I bet you made healthy choices yesterday without even realizing it! You probably ate less than you normally do, too. These things just naturally start to happen after you've been fasting for a while. Old cravings and habits begin to die.

Have another day of normal eating. Maybe, try a new food today?

## Day 24

I bet you know what's on today's agenda, don't you? Only 500 calories for women and 600 calories for men.

Go!

Stay hydrated.

## Day 25

Instead eating normally today like we did during our first round of 5:2 after a fast day, we are going for another 500 – 600 calorie day.

Keep pushing those fluids!

## Day 26

How do you feel after two days of very low calories? Record your findings in your journal.

Today, I want you to eat normally, but skip a meal and don't have any snacks. As always, you can eat what you want. Make sure you are drinking lots of fluids.

## Day 27

So, it hasn't actually been a full 5:2 plan, yet, but we are going to transition into the Warrior Diet, again.

Eat small amounts of raw fruits and veggies, dairy, and hard-boiled eggs. Drink only non-calorie beverages. Do this for 20 hours and then feast for 4 hours in the evening like a true ancient warrior.

This should be easy for you!

## Day 28

Okay, warrior! Take off your armor and do a round of Eat-Stop-Eat. No food for 24 hours.

Make sure you are drinking lots of non-calorie liquids.

## Day 29

How was your 24-hour fast? Is it getting easier to go this long without food? Go ahead and enjoy 2000 – 2500 calories, based on your gender, when your 24-hours officially ends.

You are doing amazingly well!

## Day 30

You made it! Congratulations! I'm so proud of you. Today, I want you to finish strong by skipping 2 meals. You've got this!

Make sure to weigh and measure yourself today and record your results.

What are the results of your 30 days of intermittent fasting? Even if you didn't lose an enormous amount of weight, I bet your clothes fit better. Perhaps, you feel stronger and healthier than you ever did before!

Go back over your journal notes, if you kept them, and determine which form of IF is best for you. Maybe, you'd like to stick to a mixture like we did here over the last 30 days. The choice is always yours.

# CHAPTER 3
## The Basics

In this next chapter, we are going to dive into the basics of intermittent fasting. We will talk about preparing for your fast, the types of foods and drinks you should be eating, and whether you should exercise or not.

You can use this portion of the book as a summary, or, rather, a fast track guide. We've already covered how to fast in detail. This chapter will serve as a quick reference tool for when you need a concise answer.

## The Basics of Eating While Intermittent Fasting

Intermittent fasting is not a new concept by any means. We've covered different ways of fasting that have been occurring for centuries, like The Warrior Diet. We know that fasting is a safe approach to better health and weight loss.

When we deprive ourselves of certain food groups for an extended period of time, we grow bored. That's where the "cheat days" come into play.

If you are constantly denying yourself carbohydrates and only eating meat, you're going to eventually start wishing you had bread, bagels, and potatoes. With intermittent fasting, you don't have to worry about any of that. Why? Because there are literally no food restrictions.

So, that's where I want you to start. I want you to wrap your mind around the concept of no food restrictions. Sure, in the beginning, you may find yourself binging on cakes, cookies, and pizza because it'll seem like you have a free ticket to do so. We all do it.

However, as soon as you start to adapt to IF you'll find yourself being less hungry when your eating window opens, and you'll notice that making healthier food choices will start to come naturally.

It's all psychological. Everyone wants what they can't have, but you can have it all when you choose IF as your WOE.

**Be Prepared**

Before you start your fast, make sure you have the types of food you wish to eat ready and on hand. These foods and drinks will vary depending on the type of fast you are engaging in.

For example, if you are looking to do The Warrior Diet, you'll want to have some eggs hard-boiled, some cheese slices cut up, and fresh fruits and veggies ready to go. You'll also want to have your feast food ready. I don't know about you, but when I reach the end of a long fast I want to have my favorite foods available.

There's nothing worse than getting to your feeding window and not having to eat in the house.

Make sure you have plenty of no-calorie drinks on hand. Water can get boring very quickly. If your fast permits, have black coffee, tea, and diet sodas on hand. Dr. Jason Fung says that bone broth is okay to have providing you only take it in small amounts.

## Exercise

So, food is fuel. That is basic science. What happens when you stop giving your body fuel but are still working out?

It's all about the timing.

When your body is all out of glycogen reserves, such as when you haven't consumed any food in a while, it'll find other things to use for fuel. Your body will always burn glycogen before anything else.

Some experts feel that your body will begin to burn muscle mass, however, there are a lot of folks in the medical community, like Dr. Jason Fung and Dr. Eric berg, who feel differently. Chances are, if your body isn't burning glycogen, it'll be burning ketones and then fat.

As you exercise, and you have an empty stomach, you very well may be in a state of ketosis. Here is where the whole timing thing comes into play. You really have to be fasting for at least 12 hours for this to take place. If you've eaten less than 12 hours ago and decide to workout, your body will still be using glycogen for fuel.

Here are a few tips to help you power through your workout while fasting:

1. Keep Cardio at a low level

If you are fasting, you don't want to be working out so hard that you're breathing like a fire breathing dragon. This means you are pushing yourself too hard. Going out for a light jog is acceptable. However, running a marathon while on empty will do nothing but lead to problems like fainting and feeling dizzy.

2. Save the high-intensity workout for after refeeds

When you schedule your meals around workouts you maximize your fat loss. You are also staying fueled during your workout. Try to schedule your most intense exercise routines around your last meal of the day. That way, you'll still have some glycogen available to fuel your exercise routine. You'll also lessen your risk of having your blood sugar levels bottom out. Once your high-intensity workout is complete, grab yourself a high carbohydrate snack. This will fuel your muscles.

3.  Refeed on high protein meals

If you are into serious muscle building, you'll need to consume high protein foods before and after your workout. This means more protein than just a pre-workout snack. You'll have to regularly consume protein-rich foods around the time your workout and finish working out. The Academy of Nutrition and Dietic recommends eating at least 20 to 30 grams of decent protein every 4 waking hours. You should also do this after your training program. Your refeed meals should also contain a considerable amount of protein.

These exercise regulations aren't for everyone. However, if you are into serious workout routines due to being an athlete or body builder, it is wise to understand the correlation between fasting, eating, and exercise. Doing so can greatly influence and enhance the type of muscle you build.

Please know that you do not have to incorporate exercise into your intermittent fasting routine if you don't want too. However, by doing so, you'll see quicker and more efficient results in the areas of weight loss, muscle gain, and improving health issues.

At the end of the day, even light exercise is good for your heart. Studies have shown that regular exercise is also good for your mental status. When we exercise, our brains release serotonin, the hormone that makes us feel happy and balanced.

You may wish to consider adding exercise to your IF regimen based on these facts, alone.

## Types of Foods You Should Be Eating During IF

You might be scratching your head. What types of foods do you eat during fasting? Shouldn't it be no foods? Well, the answer is actually yes and no. Obviously, you won't be consuming any foods or very much food, rather, during your fasting hours.

A "clean" fast is described as taking in no calories whatsoever. A "dirty" fast is allowing yourself small amounts of calories such as cream in your coffee or bone broth. Keep in mind, that not all fasts are the same, though.

For example, The Warrior Diet actually permits you to eat during your fast, but in small amounts and very specific food groups. This would be considered a dirty fast.

OMAD specifically says no calories of any kind for 23-hours. This is a clean fast.

There, now that we got that out of the way, what foods should you be eating if you are going to dirty fast?

- Small amounts of cream in your coffee, as in, 1-2 tsps.
- Bone broth
- Coconut oil
- MCT oil

The list doesn't stop with these foods. You can have virtually anything that you want as it is your choice. However, these are the most common foods that folks who are dirty fasting will consume. If you start eating a considerable number of calories, you aren't really fasting. Again, you must keep in mind the type of IF method you are using. Some fasts, like The Warrior Diet, are considered to be modified fasts.

What types of foods should you eat when you are not fasting? Your options are unlimited. Remember, there are no off-limit foods when you embark on an IF journey.

However, the types of foods you choose to consume during your eating window will determine how successful you are at reaching your goals. If you are looking to lose consistent, steady weight, I don't advise you to eat pizza, cake, and cookies with every meal. Yes, you might still lose weight, but it will must certainly be at a snail's pace.

If you are trying to correct health problems, you are going to want to eat a more balanced diet. Especially, people who are dealing with type 2 diabetes, high cholesterol, and high blood pressure.

**Foods to Combat Hunger**

Truthfully, limiting your intake of carbohydrates will stave off hunger pangs better than anything else. Carbohydrates turn to sugar. So, this means candy bars and bagels fall into the same category.

If you look at your plate during your feeding window and it contains mashed potatoes, a piece of pie, a dinner roll, and corn on the cob…. you're probably taking in too many carbs.

It has been proven time and time again that carbohydrates will leave you feeling satiated in the short term but will have your stomach growling in a couple of hours after consuming them.

The best thing you can do is eat a well-balanced diet that is high in non-starchy vegetables, healthy fats, and protein.

**Healthy Fats**

- Grass-fed butter
- Coconut oil
- MCT oil

- Extra-virgin olive oil
- Avocado oil
- Sesame oil
- Avocados
- Dark chocolate
- Nuts
- Chia seeds
- Cheese
- Full-fat yogurt

Try to stay away from hydrogenated and partially hydrogenated oils like soy, sunflower, and vegetable cooking oil. These oils can produce an inflammatory response in your system and can actually make issues like high cholesterol worse.

Plus, they have no nutritional value and certainly won't help to stave off hunger.

**Proteins**

- Beef
- Poultry
- Fish
- Pork
- Milk
- Beans
- Eggs

These food lists are certainly not the end all, is all of foods that can keep you feeling satiated during your fasting hours, but they are good start. You'll have to play around with what works best for you.

**Beverages to Consume While Fasting**

While you are fasting, it is pretty much agreed upon that you should only be drinking non-calorie liquids. What does this entail?

- Water
- Sparkling water
- Diet soda
- Tea
- Black coffee
- Non-calorie drink mixes
- Small amounts of bone broth
- Apple cider vinegar
- Lemon juice

Dr. Jason Fung, a pioneer in the intermittent fasting community, claims that small amounts of bone broth will not break your fast. In fact, he encourages people to drink bone broth while they are fasting because it replenishes electrolytes and is insanely good for the body. However, small amounts are key.

Apple cider vinegar has been shown to be helpful to folks who are fasting, but you should limit yourself to just 1 tbsp per day in no less than 8 ounces of water. It is very important that you dilute the apple cider vinegar in water because it can erode your teeth and even harm your esophagus if taken straight.

Lemon juice is on the same playing field as apple cider vinegar. Take no more than 1-2 tsps. in a glass of water per day. You'll find that lemon juice actually has some calories in it, so you'll want to be careful when using it during your fast.

# CHAPTER 4
# <u>TROUBLESHOOTING & FAQS</u>

We've covered a lot of ground in this book, so far. I hope you are well on your way to becoming an avid intermittent faster. However, I'm sure there are still a few stones that have been left unturned. This chapter will go over some issues you might be facing as you intermittent fast.

## Troubleshooting

### Common Mistakes of Intermittent Fasting and How to Avoid Them

You are probably excited to get started on your intermittent fasting journey. I totally understand. I was in the same position you are in, myself. I was so eager to start watching my weight fall off and to improve my health. I dove into the IF lifestyle feet first, and never looked back.

However, I made some mistakes along the way. It happens. If you are not getting the results you want, you may have to tweak a few things. Here are some troubleshooting tips to help you along the way.

### Are you jumping into IF too quickly?

As I stated above, I was super eager to hop right into an intermittent fasting lifestyle. There was no adjustment period. I just went for it. This may work for some people, but it can be an outright disaster for others.

You can't make such an extreme lifestyle change all at once. It is better to ease into IF. That's why, in the 30-day guide, I started you off with a less-intense version of IF and slowly guided you towards the more demanding methods.

If you are used to eating every couple of hours, I don't recommend that you start out with a 24-hour fast. It'll feel hellish, to be honest. You don't want to be so discouraged that you give up on IF before you've truly started.

This is the exact reason why so many people abandon their health goals so quickly after starting a new diet program. They don't ease into their new eating program and totally shock their systems.

If you are feeling overwhelmed, I suggest starting with a 12/12 program. This means you fast for 12 hours and you have a 12-hour eating window. Slowly, work your way up to 24-hours by adding another hour to your fasting schedule every couple of days.

You can also try the less intense IF methods that we mentioned in Chapter 2.

**Are you choosing the right IF method?**

If you completed my 30-day IF plan, you probably have a clear idea of which method works best for you. However, maybe you are finding that your fasting journey doesn't mesh well with your lifestyle, after all.

Work, family, school, and other aspects play a big part in the type of IF you will be successful at.

Another area to look at is how active you are. If you are an athlete, you probably don't want to fast for 23 hours a day for weeks straight. You need more calories in your life due to expending so many of them.

The same goes for leading a sedentary lifestyle. If you work a desk job, OMAD just may be the type of IF you need.

## Are you eating too much during refeeding?

This is a common mistake that many beginners make. Listen, even though there are no food restrictions, it doesn't mean you can binge eat during your eating window. If you aren't seeing the scale move, chances are you are piling your plate too high.

If you find yourself feeling terribly hungry during your fasts and all you can think about is your next meal, something isn't right. Granted, you may experience this when you're first starting out, but it is a side effect that should gradually go away.

One thing you can do is to not fast for so long. Maybe, 23 and 24 hour fasts just aren't for you. Try to do shorter fasts and eat healthy foods during your window. This might just be the answer to your binge-eating prayers.

Remember, in time, you might be ready for a longer fast, but be kind to yourself while you're adjusting.

## Are you eating enough?

We are going to swing from the other end of the pendulum, now. If you aren't losing weight, again, reevaluate your plate. If you are consuming less than 1200 calories during your refeeds (this would be all at once for 23 and 24-hour fasters and spread out over the day for other IF methods), you aren't getting enough calories.

You can actually gain weight from not eating enough. Why? Because your body will begin to cannibalize on its muscle which will cause your metabolism to slow down to a crawl. You do not want this to happen.

So, if you know beyond the shadow of a doubt that you are not eating very much during your refeed period, and you aren't losing any weight, try adding more healthy foods to your plate.

## Are you eating the right foods?

It is true that there are no dietary restrictions on what you can eat during your eating window. However, you cannot subsist on pizza, egg rolls, beer, and cake and expect to see the scale move. Sure, it might happen at first due to there being a significant calorie deficit in your routine, however, after a while this effect will subside.

You also, most assuredly, won't see any significant changes in your health, either.

If you aren't getting the results that you want, please consider the types of food you are consuming. You may just have to tweak a few things and scale back on the doughnuts, a bit.

This is not to say that you can't enjoy some fast food on the weekends or birthday cake at a party. It just means you need to eat these foods in moderation and balance your refeeds with healthy choices.

## Are you drinking enough fluids?

Did you know that when you are dehydrated you will feel hungry? Even if you are mildly thirsty, your brain is going to trick you into thinking that you are famished. This is a survival mechanism. Your body will try to get rehydrated any way that it can.

A simple way to avoid this is by keeping yourself adequately hydrated while you fast. The most important liquid you can take in is water. Pure, plain H2O.

Drinking water can prevent fatigue, muscle cramps, and hunger. If you're dealing with headaches during your fast, drink water.

Sure, you can consume other non-calorie drinks, too. However, make sure most of your daily intake of fluid is coming from water.

# IF Side Effects and How to Deal with Them

You've undoubtedly heard a ton of great things about intermittent fasting. In this book alone, we've covered how IF can help you lose weight, improve health conditions, and even let you sleep better. However, we do need to address some of the possible negative side effects.

Don't worry. When I say "negative" I mean the side effect you might experience as you are first starting out. All of these side effects can be dealt with and managed.

I feel it is only right to share what you might experience upon starting an intermittent fasting lifestyle. There is no sense in only supplying you with the good side. I want you to know what to expect so you can succeed and reach your health goals.

There are some side effects that might seem bothersome or even a little scary. You need to be prepared so you don't quit your IF journey because you think you're becoming ill.

**Feeling Hungry**

We've covered hunger throughout this entire book. I feel the need to touch base on the topic, yet again. Hunger is the most common side effect that anyone embarking on an IF lifestyle will feel. It just happens.

When you are used to eating throughout the day and you suddenly stop doing so, your body is going to become confused and wonder what on earth is going on. Your system has become accustomed to expecting food at certain times. When food isn't given, your body releases a hormone called, ghrelin.

You know when your stomach starts to growl? Yep, that's ghrelin at work. This is why most Americans feel hungry upon waking, at noon, and in the evening. We are used to eating our 3 square meals a day. IF totally changes this.

Please know, and be prepared for, levels of ghrelin to increase when you first start fasting. This means you are going to feel hungrier than ever before. It's normal and it is temporary.

You are going to need quite a bit of self-control, especially on days 3 to 5. These are the days that ghrelin is going to be at its highest point. Don't give in to ghrelin.

If you feed your hunger pangs you will essentially be starting the entire process over. Your body will learn to adapt to your new IF lifestyle and your hunger pangs will start to subside.

One of things you can do to deal with the crazy hunger you are feeling is to drink a ton of water. Each time you feel a hunger pang, down 12 oz. or more of water. Doing this will tell your brain that your stomach is full, and ghrelin doesn't need to be released any longer.

**Having Cravings**

Whenever we deny ourselves something, that is typically the thing we crave. If I told you that you could never eat a piece of cheese again (oh, the horror!), you'd probably not be able to stop thinking about cheese.

During fasting, you are telling yourself that you cannot have food, of any kind, for a certain set of hours. So, naturally, you're going to be craving all sorts of things to eat. You may even find yourself craving something like celery, because, well, it is food.

I find that the best way to avoid craving food is to not think about food. How does one do that? By keeping yourself busy.

Work, study, sing, dance, take up a hobby. These are just some of the things you can do to avoid having thoughts of food.

Remember, cravings are a mind over matter type of thing. You can tell yourself that you can have that grilled cheese sandwich, but it has to be in a few hours. You can do this!

**Headaches**

Unfortunately. Headaches can be a side effect of intermittent fasting. There are two main reasons behind this. One reason is the lack of sugar you are consuming. When you fast for significant periods of time, you aren't taking in carbohydrates. Carbs turn into sugar in our bloodstream.

Carb/sugar addiction is VERY real. A side effect of sugar withdrawal is having headaches. This side effect typically subsides as your body adjusts. You can help it along even quicker by not eating a ton of carbs during your refeed period.

Another reason behind headaches and fasting is not staying adequately hydrated. If you aren't taking in enough fluids, you are at risk for dehydration. A side effect of this is having a pounding head.

Make sure to drink plenty of water and other non-caloric beverages.

**Having No Energy**

Because your body is no longer in a constant fed state, your energy levels can plummet. Again, this is only temporary and will improve in time. Many experts suggest not starting a workout program until your body becomes more adjusted to IF.

I totally agree with them.

Try to keep your day as stress-free and low-key as possible for a few weeks after starting IF.

If you were working out prior to IF, consider stopping for a few weeks or lighten up your routine. This will help keep those sluggish feelings at bay.

Walking and yoga are wonderful examples of light exercise.

**Feeling Cranky**

You've probably heard the term "hangry" before. If you haven't, it is a play on the words hungry and angry, thus creating, hangry. When we are hungry, and our hunger need isn't being met, we can become irritable.

This is mainly due to your blood sugars dropping.

Unfortunately, there isn't much you can do to combat feeling irritable during fasting other than staying out of situations that annoy you. Once again, as you become more accustomed to fasting, your crankiness will decrease.

Try not to focus on the negatives of life and look for those little gems of everyday joy.

**Heartburn**

This side effect isn't as common as the others, but it does affect certain people. If you already deal with acid reflux, intermittent fasting could make your symptoms worse, but only temporarily.

You might feel mild discomfort to full on pain. You may even notice that you are belching more frequently than you used to. This is all normal. However, if it becomes to bothersome, stop fasting and consult your doctor.

To lessen the symptoms of heartburn, you can avoid spicy and greasy foods during your feeding window. You can also drink more water and sleep in a more upright position.

## Constipation and Belly Bloat

Some folks become constipated during intermittent fasting. This can be due to the lack of food in your daily intake. It can also be from not eating enough fibrous foods and/or drinking enough water.

If you are having trouble moving your bowels, try adding more raw fruits and vegetables to your eating window. Make sure you are drinking plenty of water, too.

Speaking of water, if you are experiencing belly bloat, water can significantly help relieve your symptoms. Having consistent bowel movements will also lessen your bloating issues.

## Feeling Cold

A lot of people have cold hands and feet while they fast. This can be a good thing! Did you know that when you fast, blood circulation increases to your fat reserves? Yep! This is referred to as, "adipose tissue blood flow". When this happens, your fat stores are being moved to your muscles?

So, does this mean your muscles will become flabby? No!

It means that your fat will be used as fuel and you will burn it off. When you your hands and feet feel cold during fasting you can sit back and smile because you know your fat is being melted away.

Another reason why your fingertips and toes might be feeling a little icy is due to the decrease in your blood sugar. This is normal.

You can warm up by sipping on hot tea, taking a bubble bath, and wearing warmer clothing.

## Binge Eating

It is a common thing for people just starting out on IF to overeat during their feeding window. This can happen because you have gotten it into your head that there are no food restrictions on IF and you can basically have your own buffet when it is time to chow down.

Yep, you are right, there are no food restrictions when engaging in an IF lifestyle, but as I've stated many times before, you cannot go overboard. It isn't healthy, and it isn't going to help you meet your weight loss goals any time soon.

Another reason why people overeat on IF is because they are still adjusting to not eating every couple of hours. When their window opens, they go crazy and act as if they have been starved on an island for 30 days.

If you are finding this happening to you, consider shortening up the length of your fasts and gradually increasing them over time. This will help you to not feel so famished.

What it essentially boils down to is self-control. You might feel like eating several pieces of pizza at the end of your fast, but you need to ask yourself, "Do I really need, too"?

**Increased Urination**

Are you finding yourself running to the toilet more often since starting IF? Good! That means you've been drinking ample amounts of fluids.

Honestly, there is no way to slow down your bathroom visits unless you stop drinking so much water and other healthy fluids. You and I both know that is not an option.

Make sure to stock your bathroom with plenty of good reading material. ☺

**Listen to Your Body**

I understand that these side effects sound pretty intense. You may even be reconsidering IF altogether. Please understand, these side effects only last a couple of weeks until your body adjusts. Some people don't experience any side effects at all.

Now, if you are feeling truly terrible and your symptoms aren't improving, by all means, stop fasting and go see your doctor. You know your body better than anyone. If it is telling you to stop, listen.

I will say that I have experienced quite a few of the listed side effects and they only lasted about a week into my IF journey. The key is taking good care of yourself. Drink plenty of water, get fresh air, and make sure you are sleeping well.

Remember, having a positive mindset is one of the most important parts of being successful during IF.

# FAQS

In this section, we will go over some of the most frequently asked questions about intermittent fasting. I know we have covered a lot of ground this far, but perhaps you have a burning question that hasn't yet been addressed. Hopefully, you'll find the answer, here.

**Which method of intermittent fasting should you follow?**

This is a question that you need to ask yourself. I can't tell you which method of IF is going to work out best for your current situation because I don't know your lifestyle. However, I encourage you to follow the 30-day IF guide and try out the 7 most popular types of IF for yourself.

Maybe one of them will work amazingly well for you or you might wish to incorporate a mixture of IF methods into your life.

Things to consider are your current weight loss goals, your health goals, your job, your activity level, and whether or not you are brand new to intermittent fasting.

**What should you eat during your feeding window?**

There are no restrictions when it comes to what you can and cannot eat during your refeed periods. However, as we've discussed throughout this entire book, it is not a free-for-all, either.

If you want to live off pizza and ice cream during your eating window, go for it. You just need to be prepared for a lack of weight loss and your health issues to not be addressed.

If you are looking to eat in a way that'll compliment your health and weight loss goals, incorporate a balance of healthy carbs, proteins, fruits and veggies, and dairy into your routine. Make sure to drink plenty of water and other non-calorie containing beverages.

Keep in mind, you can still have processed foods, sweets, and whatever else you crave, but try to eat them in moderation. These foods should not be making up your entire meal on a regular basis.

**What is the impact of Circadian Rhythms on fasting?**

Basically, circadian rhythms are predictable, 24-hour natural changes that occur within our bodies. These changes impact our behaviors, hormones, and glandular activity, amongst other things. Many of the hormones in the body such as human growth hormone, cortisol, and parathyroid hormone are secreted during the circadian rhythm cycle.

Did you know that these rhythms have evolved over the ages to accurately respond to the way our bodies perceive light, seasons, and the times of day? All of these things tell your body how readily available food is. These types of patterns are seen in both animals and humans. Studies have shown that 10% of any given organism's cellular makeup show changes within their circadian rhythms.

There is a little something called the suprachiasmatic nucleus (SCN), otherwise known as the master circadian clock. This element is believed to tell our bodies when food is available and when it is not. For example, during the Paleolithic era, food was relatively scarce during the daylight hours. This is because the people of that time were out hunting and gathering food during the day and feasting on what they found during the evening hours.

Most modern humans will eat their meals throughout the day because unlike our ancestors, food is always readily available to us. With the exception of some nocturnal animals and those who work a third shift job, rarely do life forms eat during the night.

Natural circadian hunger does exist. Studies have shown that your hunger levels are lowest in the morning after you wake up. This is interesting because you'd think, after going without food all night long, you'd be famished in the morning. This simply is not true. In fact, people who do enjoy breakfast typically eat a much smaller amount of food during this meal than they do at lunch or dinner.

This shows us that based on circadian rhythms, fasting doesn't increase your hunger, eating does. Did you know that hunger typically falls to its lowest level just before 8:00 am? This is when your body makes the least of the hormone known as "ghrelin".

Basically, you want to eat your largest meal during the mid-day hours. This would be between noon and 3:00 pm. Granted, not everyone is the same, nor are we all able to make this time period our eating window. However, if you find you are struggling with overbearing hunger pangs during your fasts, try eating between

12 and 3 pm to see if your body responds better to the circadian rhythm cycle.

**How do you safely break your fast?**

I know you have been fasting for hours and you are ready to tear up that Chinese buffet. Put the brakes on for a minute, tiger.

Look, you've been fasting for quite a while. You can't start dumping food into your system like nobody's business. You need to take it slow. Yes, you can have the Chinese buffet, but there are a few steps you need to take before diving into the wontons.

Here are some great foods to break your fast gently with:

- Fruit and veggie juices
- Raw fruits
- Bone broth
- Yogurt
- Green, leafy vegetables
- Steamed veggies
- Veggie soup
- Raw veggies
- Cooked whole grains
- Cooked beans
- Nuts
- Eggs
- Dairy products
- Meat

If you've been on a long fast, I suggest breaking it with the first three foods on the list. You can gradually add in some of the others afterward.

Now, if you have only been fasting a few hours, there is no need to "safely" break the fast. This section pertains to extended fasters, only.

**Fasting and Bodybuilding**

Honestly, it is no secret that intermittent fasting helps you to build muscle, tone up, and look fit. This is why so many body builders are in the business of fasting. There are a ton of weight training programs out there that promote fasting and only consuming things like water, various juices, and other very low-calories foods and drinks. Body builders will typically follow this strict period of fasting with a large feast as part of their training routine.

Did you know that consuming just water alone during your fast helps your body to cleanse itself better than if you were eating small amounts of low-calorie food and drinks? You are literally rattled with impurities and a clean fast is the best way to rid yourself of them. Some bodybuilders and athletes take this approach for the sole purpose of detoxing their bodies.

In fact, in some cultures, like the Chinese, fasting is just a way of life for everyone. Even people who are athletic and fit will partake in some form of fasting. I mean, how do you think they stay fit and toned and strong? Certainly not by eating every few hours of the day.

Anyway, body building and fasting are closely related to one another. Did you know that in order to build the body up you need your body to be in a state of physical fitness? Some who is extremely out of shape and wants to transform into a bodybuilder has a long road ahead of them. Before they can even think about gaining some bulky muscles, they need to get their health on track, first. This can be done by driving away toxins from the body by doing clean, water fasts.

Plus, by engaging in a clean, water fast, the future bodybuilder is giving their vital organs a much-needed rest because they won't be digesting food all of the time.

Here are some things to keep in mind as you set out on your fasting and bodybuilding journey:

- As a beginner, you or your friends may think that intermittent fasting and bodybuilder sounds a bit ludicrous. You may even find yourself wanting to give up due to lack of support from your peers. Don't do it! Educate yourself on why intermittent fasting and bodybuilding works. In order to get the type of results you want, you must persevere.
- Don't fall into the trap of going overboard with your fast and workout schedule. Start out slowly and work your way up to more severe fasts and exercise regimens. You don't want to stress your body out. Your goal is to heal your body, so you can start to gain lean muscle mass.
- Make sure you pay attention to your body's cues. If you feel like you're doing too much too quickly, scale it back a little. There's nothing wrong with slow and steady results.

Know that if you are pushing yourself to the max with fasting and weightlifting or cardio and you start to feel a little fatigued or worn out, slow down. Eat something very small, if you need to. Yes, this will break your fast, but it is better than gorging yourself on a high calorie food.

When it becomes time to break your fast, start out with a small meal and gradually work your way up to a heartier portion. There is no sense in fasting and training for a substantial amount of time and then binging on excessive calories all at once.

For people who aren't bodybuilders, this can be okay, but for the serious athlete who is training, it is definitely not okay.

Did you know that fasting and bodybuilding have gone hand in hand for decades? In fact, it is one of the oldest methods of ridding your body of toxins in an almost 100% effective way. Once you get your body into proper condition, it is important to ensure that it stays there. Bodybuilding will definitely put you on the track to long-term health and wellness, not to mention you'll look fit and fabulous.

Bodybuilding and fasting not only helps your physical appearance but it also improves your confidence. You won't be afraid to look in the mirror, anymore. You'll feel healthy and strong. All of these things will lift your mood and help balance out your emotions. Above all else, you'll know the value of food and how important it is to not abuse it.

Fasting helps you to form one of the integral building blocks of the bodybuilding industry. Your body will be conditioned by the fasting and ready to take on all the stresses that bodybuilding will put onto it. When I say stresses, I don't necessarily mean that in a bad way. We just know that bodybuilding isn't easy, and it can be taxing on the body so that is why it is so important to be in shape before you start. Fasting can help you get there and help you maintain the lean muscle gains you've created on the way.

There is plenty of proof that intermittent fasting and bodybuilding complement one another. For example, Sergio Nubret is one of the most amazing and successful bodybuilders of all time. This man wholeheartedly believes in the power of fasting and bodybuilding. Mr. Nubret has an amazing body and he got through fasting and hard work. We can all learn something from this man.

Did you know that Sergio Nubret ate like a wild grizzly bear? No, this man didn't go around finding unsuspecting humans to devour. However, during his refeed window, he ate piles and piles of food, consuming thousands of calories. Granted, if you aren't a bodybuilder, you certainly cannot do this. However, the serious bodybuilder needs far more calories than the average Joe.

The intermittent fasting method that Sergio Nubret used was the one meal a day approach, otherwise known as OMAD. He essentially packed 4 meals a day into a 1-hour eating window. That's pretty impressive! Now, again, this type of eating regimen is not for people who aren't into bodybuilding. You'd be on the fast track to weight gain in no time if you lead a sedentary lifestyle and eat like a wild grizzly bear.

If you are into bodybuilding and wish to try fasting, you need a calorie surplus to build your muscles. This means that it doesn't matter how many meals you consume in a 24-hour period. All that matters is whether you're left with a calorie surplus or not. If you are in the throes of heavy weight training, you need those extra calories to build and maintain your muscles. This is why fasting and bodybuilding work so beautifully, together.

Just like Sergio Nubret's story, there are plenty of other well-known folks who have used fasting and bodybuilding to gain the physique that most people crave. Brad Pilon and John Berardi name a couple.

Adding fasting to your bodybuilding journey may or may not be the right approach for you. However, the only way that you will know is by testing the theory out for yourself.

## Will you lose muscle?

Truthfully, everyone loses a bit of muscle mass when the start a new diet. The concern is how much muscle you lose and if you continue to lose muscle.

If the majority of your refeed meals are made up of balanced foods and you are staying adequately hydrated, you shouldn't have any problems with significant muscle loss.

Keeping your metabolism working well is another way to avoid muscle loss.

Aim for slow, consistent weight loss and your muscles shouldn't be affected any more than any other diet program. When rapid weight loss happens, this is where muscle mass loss is affected the most.

## How do you refeed when you aren't fasting to lose weight?

If you are someone who does not have a goal of weight loss in mind and simply wish to maintain your current weight, fasting can still work for you. You'll reap all of the benefits of fasting like autophagy, which is a plus.

Basically, to keep yourself from losing weight, make sure your refeed meals never fall below 1800 calories. You'll have to figure out how to get these calories based upon the IF method you choose to follow.

## Why would you fast if you don't wish to lose weight?

Fasting is so much more than weight loss. In the long run, you'll improve your overall health, combat sugar addiction, and help yourself develop a better relationship with food.

There are a ton of people who have reversed significant health problems by implementing intermittent fasting into their life. For some, weight loss is just a bonus.

**How do you match your workout sessions with your fasting schedule?**

If You are an athlete or in any type of training program, it is advised that you center your meals around your workout. You should eat protein before your workout and as a main source of fuel during your refeed meals.

It is also suggested that you eat some type of carbohydrate directly after your workout as this will refuel your muscles.

**Are you able to drink diet soda during your fasts?**

Sure, there is really no reason why you can't have diet soda drinks when you fast. But you need to bear in mind that artificial sweeteners can make some people feel hungry. This has to do with your mouth tasting something sweet and your brain releasing an insulin response to the rest of your body with the anticipation of impending sugar.

You'll just have to experiment with diet drinks and see how they affect you on an individual basis.

**Should you take vitamins and supplements while you fast?**

The short answer is yes and no.

Basically, it boils down to WHEN you take your vitamins and supplements. Some vitamins and supplements contain quite a bit of calories. You should take them during your eating window.

Something to keep in mind is some vitamins actually work better when taken with food. Almost all multi-vitamins have a better absorption rate when consumed while eating a meal.

You can take things like probiotics and various herbs outside of your eating window, if you prefer.

## How should you prepare for intermittent fasting?

One of the first things you want to do before starting an intermittent fasting program is to go see your doctor. Discuss with him or her your plans to intermittent fast and why you want to do it. Be open to what your doctor has to say.

Ask your doctor for a complete medical workup that includes blood work and urinalysis. You want to have a baseline of where you stand in terms of your health.

Once you get the green light from your health care professional, go grab yourself a journal. Write down your "why". List out your goals and how you plan to reach them. I'd visit this journal everyday while you are in the starting stages of IF.

You'll want to stock your pantry and refrigerator with approved fasting foods. Now, this only pertains to the folks who are engaging in the short fasting window methods or The Warrior Diet. You want to make sure you have everything you need on hand.

Make a meal plan and grocery list for your feast meals. This will help you to binge less. If you are planning on following a special diet for your fest meals, make sure you have regular meals planned for your family.

Just because you are intermittent fasting and trying to eat a healthier diet does not mean everyone else has, too. I know it makes your health goals even harder but you're only in control of yourself.

Make sure you have plenty of water, coffee, tea, diet soda, and other non-calorie drinks on hand.

Find things to do during your fasting hours so that you stay busy. This will help with hunger pangs and cravings. Maybe you'll want to join a yoga class, grab a new book, or take up knitting. Do what will help you succeed.

Self-talk is a wonderful tool to utilize. Prepare yourself for fasting by speaking positive affirmations. Start each day with looking in the mirror and telling yourself that you can do this because you are smart and have self-control.

**Will you get headaches while fasting?**

You may. Not everyone experiences this side effect, but many people do. This is because of lack of sugar in the bloodstream and not getting enough water. As we have discussed earlier in this book, most people are addicted to sugar. Removing sugar from your diet through fasting will insight a withdrawal response. Headaches are a symptom of withdrawal. Don't worry, they'll go away as your body adjusts.

Make sure you are drinking plenty of water to keep yourself hydrated. Being hydrated helps stave away headaches.

If your head is really hurting, you can try drinking a cup of black coffee as caffeine can helps with head pain, too.

**Will your body go into starvation mode when intermittent fasting?**

No. Let's be clear on what starvation actually is. When your body has run out of both external and stored nutrient and energy sources, you're starving. This is when the body starts to cannibalize on itself.

Will this happen during intermittent fasting? Probably not. The reason I say "probably" is because there are people out there who simply should not be fasting. Those folks fall into the underweight, undernourished, and unhealthy category.

For everyone else, who is a healthy adult, IF will not put you into "starvation mode".

Think of it this way, have you ever seen an overweight person die of starvation? No! Whenever we see pictures of people that have died of starvation they are emaciated.

You won't be fasting to the point of emaciation on IF. That's just not how it works.

**If you're a woman, can you safely intermittently fast?**

Absolutely! The only time a woman should not fast is when she is trying to get pregnant, is already pregnant, or she is breastfeeding a baby. Aside from other medical problems that she and her doctor have deemed as no-goes for fasting, women are welcome to fast just like their male counterparts.

Bear in mind that women need less calories than men during their refeeds, unless of course, you are a woman who partakes in extreme athletics and training programs.

You may notice some changes in your menstrual cycle when you first begin to fast, but these changes are typically temporary.

If a woman is interested in weight loss, she should seriously consider intermittent fasting. Women should ignore the stigma surrounding intermittent fasting and what other people think that they know and go with an eating plan that has been proven to work for just about any human. There are many studies to prove that intermittent fasting helps women lose weight and keep it off, in a safe manner.

Some folks may think that intermittent fasting is a new trend that women are jumping on the bandwagon for. This simply isn't true. Women have been fasting for thousands of years, just like men.

A great place for women to start is with Alternate Day fasting. Granted, if you need to make some modifications to this diet, by all means, go for it. The American Journal of Clinical Nutrition actually did a study of Alternate Day fasting and how it affected both men and women during a 10-week cycle.

During the fasting days, the subjects ate food that made up of 25% of their normal daily intake. On the opposite days, they ate whatever they wanted. There where nutritionists available to recommend healthy food choices to the subjects, but essentially, they ate what the felt like eating.

As the medical community expected, the subjects all lost weight using Alternate Day fasting, especially the women. Not only did the ladies lose more weight but their cholesterol levels, triglycerides, and systolic pressures improved, too!

This study alone encouraged more women to try fasting and for good reason!

There are so many beneficial aspects of intermittent fasting for women. Unlike men, women have more body fat. This is due to being made to carry babies. Women don't want to lose too much of their body fat or they can see issues arise with their reproductive health. Alternate Day fasting is a gentle, yet effective way for women to safely lose weight and not infringe upon their fat reserves that are meant for pregnancy.

Did you know that when trying to lose weight, especially in women, the body will burn through its sugar stores within the first 6 hours of fasting? Then it goes to burning pure body fat. Women who are following a standard diet and/or exercising may not see this effect. However, if they start intermittent fasting, they will soon lapse into ketosis and start burning fat away like a roaring fire.

Now, women's bodies are made differently than men, for a host of reasons. There are significant changes that a woman goes through once she hits her menopause years. One of the biggest changes that women in this season of life face is they start to gain weight. This is due to their metabolism starting to slow down. Fasting can be a wonderful way to get your menopausal metabolism slump back in the game, again.

There have been plenty of studies to show that fasting helps women to regulate their appetites and people who follow a regular fasting routine tend to experience fewer cravings than people who do not fast. If you are a woman who is over the age of 50 and are dealing with weight gain and food cravings, consider giving fasting a shot. It could literally change everything for you. Plus, it is said that fasting is anti-aging. Wouldn't you want to look younger than your friends who are going through menopause, too? I bet fasting can even make you look younger than your friends and family members who actually are younger than you.

Remember, once you approach your fifties, you are more susceptible to a host of different things like chronic illnesses, high cholesterol, high blood pressure, and even skin changes. Intermittent fasting helps you combat these things with gusto. Fasting can help you get wayward LDL cholesterol and high blood pressure under control, even if you don't lose weight.

**Is fasting doable when on vacation?**

Yes! It might be a little harder than if you were at home, but you can totally do it. It's all about your mindset.

You can also adjust the method of fasting that you wish to do to be a better fit for a vacation. Maybe try the 5:2 method. You can eat normally while on your vacation for 5 days and then only consume 500-600 calories for 2 days when you get home, assuming your vacation is only a week long.

## Are all people good candidates for an intermittent fasting lifestyle?

If you are over the age of 18, healthy, well-nourished, and do not suffer from any eating disorders, then yes, you are able to fast.

After you start fasting is when you'll really know if it is right for you.

Keep in mind that women who are trying to conceive, are pregnant, or nursing a child are not good candidates for fasting.

If you have medical issues that your doctor has determined put you at risk during fasting, you are not a good candidate.

## Is intermittent fasting a good long-term solution for your weight loss goals?

Yes, it absolutely is. IF is a lifestyle, not a diet. When you decide to utilize intermittent fasting as a way to lose weight, you should be in it for the long haul.

If you go back to eating all the time, you'll gain all of your weight back and then some. The key to keeping your weight off is continuing to do what you did to lose it in the first place.

This is why intermittent fasting works because at least some form of it is able to be done for the rest of your life.

## Should you follow a ketogenic diet while intermittent fasting?

You certainly do not have to follow a ketogenic diet while intermittent fasting, but many people claim that it does help them reach their goals, faster.

Keto is the process of significantly lowering your intake of carbohydrates and increasing the amount of healthy fat that you eat.

There have been plenty of studies conducted to show that sugar makes you fat, not fat.

Personally, I do follow a ketogenic diet during my refeeds. It has been very helpful for me to meet my weight loss goals and to combat some health issues I was having.

Keto will help you get over sugar addiction much quicker than fasting alone. Plus, fat is satiating. If you are cutting out carbs and replacing them with healthy fats, you'll most likely not deal with horrible hunger pangs and cravings.

However, following a ketogenic diet is not required of intermittent fasting and you certainly do not have to do it if it does not suit you.

**What are the biggest benefits of intermittent fasting?**

There are literally tons of benefits from utilizing IF. Many of them are 100% backed by science, too. People choose to incorporate IF into their lifestyles because they want to improve their health, lose weight, and feel better.

Check out some of the benefits you can notice when you add IF to your routine:

1. Increased life expectancy
2. Hormonal profile improvements
3. Weight loss
4. Maintenance of skeletal muscle mass
5. Decrease in blood glucose levels
6. Increase in insulin sensitivity
7. Increase in lipolysis
8. Increase in fat oxidation
9. Increase in uncoupling pretein-3 mRNA
10. Increase in certain hormones that break down fat

11. Increase in growth hormone levels which help you keep your muscle mass from breaking down

**Why does fasting work to burn fat and help you to lose weight?**

When you don't eat your body has to rely on its fat stores. It really is that simple. When you are eating, your body is going to burn glycogen for fuel before anything else. Why? Because if your insulin levels get too high, you'll die.

**Will fasting cause hair loss?**

Some people have found that when they begin any new dieting program, their hair starts to fall out. This is usually due to the process of losing weight.

It may seem like you are losing a lot of hair but don't fret. This side effect is temporary and usually stops after your body adjusts to fasting and weight loss.

If the issue persists, please, consult your health care provider.

**Do the hours that you sleep count towards your fast?**

Yes! The 100% do. If you eat a snack right before bed, go to sleep, and wake up 8 hours later, you're already 8 hours into your fast. Pretty neat, eh?

That's why I advise people who are utilizing the 16:8 plan to stop eating at 8pm and resume eating at noon the next day. Half of the battle has been won while they're asleep.

**Can you add cream to your coffee or tea during your fasting hours?**

If you are adding calories to your coffee or tea, then you are breaking your fast. However, Dr. Jason Fung says that a teaspoon or 2 of cream isn't going to hurt you.

If you need to add tiny amount of cream to your coffee to get you through your day, do it. I'd rather see you have a teaspoon of cream than get so out of sorts that you end up eating a candy bar.

**Isn't skipping breakfast bad for you?**

It is true, we've been ingrained by our mothers and grandmas to never skip breakfast. How many times have you been told that breakfast is what fuels you for the rest of the day?

Honestly, you can skip breakfast through intermittent fasting and be perfectly fine, all day long. In fact, many people report being more focused and having a clearer mind when they are starting the day off by digesting.

Remember, nobody ever lost any weight by consuming more calories. This includes eating your breakfast.

**Do you need to exercise while intermittent fasting in order to lose weight?**

Honestly? No, you do not need to exercise while intermittent fasting to lose weight. However, this isn't to say that regular exercise is not good for you, because it is. Most doctors recommend that you workout most days of the week for health purposes. Exercising helps to keep your heart healthy.

With all of that being said, if you are solely utilizing intermittent fasting to lose weight, you do not need to workout to accomplish this. Intermittent fasting does not require you to physically exert yourself like exercising does. All you need to do is not eat for a period of time and then start eating again. That's it! That's the mechanics of intermittent fasting. There is no exercise needed to lose weight utilizing this dietary method.

To have some marked weight loss, swiftly and quickly, you can begin with 24-hour fasts just once or twice a week. This is a good way to get your metabolism built up and to get your feet wet in the world of fasting, if you are new to it. You will lose weight and never have to step foot in the gym. Isn't that crazy? Sounds like a pretty good deal if you ask me! Not only will this save you a ton of time but money, as well. You don't have to purchase a gym membership, gym clothes, or spend the gas money to get to the gym. You also don't need to make special time allotments for going to the gym or working out someplace else, either. This can be a wonderful thing for the busy mom or dad who has to devote their time to raising kids and not working out.

The fasting method focuses on what you put in your mouthy versus how much you are working out, in terms of weight loss. Truthfully, 90% of weight loss is centered around food, not exercise. When trying to lose fat, diet and nutrition should make up most of your program. You should not be relying on some tired old workout routine that sucks your energy, time, and money. Working out without watching what and when you eat will never produce the results you are looking for and they certainly won't help you maintain any progress that you did manage to achieve. Your diet is directly linked to your blood hormones levels and these are the hormones that determine how much fat loss you'll see.

During fasting, you'll create a calorie deficit. This is what essentially leads to weight loss and lasting fat loss. It really does not matter how you create this deficit, just as long as it exists. You can do this through fasting alone.

Now, I want to reiterate that exercise is not a bad thing, it is just not a requirement for fat loss during fasting. However, when fasting and exercise are combined, you can expect to see weight loss happen a little quicker. Exercise will also help your health problems improve, too.

Did you know that when you work out, the levels of insulin within your blood stream start to balance out? Your human growth hormone levels will increase, and this promotes weight loss. Now, in order to loss fat, these two things need to occur. As we've talked about above, fasting can make them happen all on its own. Exercise, on the other hand, will help these occurrences take place a little faster.

Studies have shown that clean fasting (nothing but water) for 24-hours can create the same hormonal blood levels that working out does. So, if you fasted just once or twice a week for around 24-hours a pop, you could replicate the effects that working out does without having to ever step foot in a gym.

This is really good news for people who can't stand working out!

**Is intermittent fasting really as amazing as it sounds?**

Yes, I certainly think that it is. I wouldn't have written this book if I wasn't completely smitten by intermittent fasting. Let's take a look at why this method of weight loss, fat loss, and health improvement is so stunning:

- **You get to eat when and what you want**

Are you a night eater? Great! Break your fast during the evening hours. Do you hate breakfast? No problem! Make the morning hours part of your fasting time. You can eat what you want when you break your fast, even if it is a juicy hamburger from your favorite fast food joint, once in a while.

- **Boost your self esteem**

One of the biggest aspects of intermittent fasting for me is how people react when they see me. You see, I spent some time being overweight. Once I started intermittent fasting, my body started changing and people noticed. There is nothing better than people who haven't seen you in a long time saying, "Wow! You look great! Have you lost weight"? Your clothes will start to fit looser, and you'll begin liking what you see in the mirror.

- **Your brain will find its serotonin**

Once your body has gotten rid of all of its impurities and toxins through fasting, you'll notice that you will begin to feel happier. The depression will begin to lift, and you'll start to have some pep in your step, once again. If you have been taking antidepressants, you might not even need them anymore. Of course, don't go getting off your medication without your doctors' consent.

- **Fasting for just 3 months can produce some remarkable effects**

If you really want to see all of the amazing things intermittent fasting can do for you, give it a go for at least 90 days. This is the timeframe in which most people see marked results. Your health should be better, you should be slimmer, and your overall mood will undoubtedly be lifted.

I hope these FAQS helped answer some of your burning questions. I know that when I first started IF I was full of questions. I kept a very good friend of mine, who practiced IF, on her toes. She could pretty much bet on the fact that it was me calling whenever she heard her phone ring.

Know that there is nothing wrong with asking questions. It's how we learn. I want you to be successful on your IF journey. Knowledge is power.

# CHAPTER 5
# IF HACKS & TIPS

There are many different ways to make your intermittent fasting lifestyle easier. Don't feel that you have follow this way of eating by the textbook rules. What works for someone else may not work for you, and that's okay.

In this next chapter we are going to focus on some hacks and tips that will help make your IF journey the best that it can be.

## Tips and Tricks

### How to easily portion your food

Did you know that your hand can be a great way to portion out your food? If you don't have measuring cups and spoons available, or you simply do not want to use them, that's okay. Your hand will work just fine.

- Your fist is great for measuring out 1 cup of food
- The thumb (from tip to the first joint) can be used for measuring out 1 teaspoon of sauce, dressing, or oil
- The entire thumb is great for measuring out ounces, such as a slice of cheese
- Use your flattened palm to measure out 3 ounces
- Your cupped hands hold 1 to 2 ounces depending on their size

You can also use various items around the house to measure your food.

- A deck of playing cards amount to about 3 ounces

- A baseball is the equivalent to 1 cup of pasta
- A tennis ball equals ½ cup of fruit
- 4 playing dice equal 1.5 ounces of cheese
- 1 die equals 1 teaspoon of cream cheese or butter

**How to save time and money while meal prepping**

Meal prepping, whether you are an intermittent faster or not, is a great way to cut down on your time in the kitchen and save you some money. Even with IF, meal prepping is a wise choice to make because you still need to eat after your fast. Some of you have families to prepare food for, too.

When I first started intermittent fasting and following the keto diet, my family wanted nothing to do with it. So, I had to make two meals, one for them and one for myself. Meal prepping was a life saver.

Here a few steps to making meal prepping a success:

1. **Plan your meals** – Sitting down at the table with pen and paper and your smartphone can help you successfully plan your meals for the week. Some folks even plan for the entire month. You can also pull out some of those cookbooks you have collecting dust on your shelf and pick meals from them, too.
   Write down the days of the week on your paper and add a meal you wish to prepare next to each day. Once you've chosen your meals, Flip the paper over, and start making out your grocery list.
   Take your list with you to the store and stick to it. Tell yourself, "If it isn't on the list, I'm not buying it".

2. **Make wise choices** – If you plan to meal prep for a long duration, like the entire month, choose meals that freeze, easily. You'll be cooking these meals in advance and

placing them into the freezer. This makes life so much easier when you are fasting. When you've fasted all day and you are hungry, the last thing you want to do is take the time to cook a meal.

By having already prepared meals, you will be less apt to ordering unhealthy takeout or binge eating. Plus, this method works out fabulously if you have a family to feed, too.

3. **Begin meal prepping** – Now, you're going to pick a day to do your meal prep. Depending on how long you plan to prep for, this could turn into an all-day cooking extravaganza. Plan accordingly.

    On this day, you'll want to cook your meat, boil your rice, chop up your fruits and veggies, etc. Once that is done, you'll start assembling your meals. By the end of the prep period, you'll be able to place all of the meals into freezer-safe containers and put them into the freezer. Make sure to label and date each one of your meals.

**Here are some meal prepping hacks:**

- Look for simple meals. Overly complicated meals, like rack of lamb, do not prep well and they certainly don't save you any money
- Try to cook 2 different dinners at once by dividing your baking pan with foil and creating an individual pouch for each meal. You can do this with the slow cooker, too
- Keep portions small so that they reheat better. For example, don't freeze an entire cooked chicken but rather cut it into portion sizes

- If any of your meals requires significantly wet ingredients, consider leaving them out until you are ready to serve the meal. This will keep your food from becoming soggy
- Place all of your prepped foods into clear containers and bags so they are easy to identify
- Try and plan your meal prep day on the weekends. This helps you to not be bothered or distracted by the comings and goings of the busy work and school week

**Nutrient Dense Food Swaps**

Even though there are no food restriction when following an intermittent fasting lifestyle, you still want to eat foods that are rich in vitamins and minerals. Occasionally, swapping out one food for a healthier version is wise. Here, you find a list of healthy food swaps that'll make getting nutrient dense foods into your diet easier.

**Cashew Cheese**

You can swap out dairy cheese for cashew cheese in a variety of ways. I've found that cashew cheese makes a killer substitute for mozzarella. You can use cashew cheese as a spread, dip, and even stirred into pasta sauces.

Cashew cheese contains a great deal of healthy fats, magnesium, and protein. It can also benefit your heart.

**Apple Cider Vinegar**

Not all apple cider vinegar is created equally. You want to choose one that contains "The Mother". I prefer using Braggs Apple Cider

Vinegar, the best. It is raw and unfiltered and definitely contains The Mother.

You can use apple cider vinegar in place of salad dressing, balsamic vinegar, or red wine vinegar.

Apple cider vinegar is loaded with gut-loving bacteria and prebiotics.

**Tahini**

You can use tahini as a suitable replacement for peanut butter. Now, don't get me wrong, there isn't anything horrible about peanut butter, but sometimes, it contains a lot of sugar and carbohydrates.

People who are following a ketogenic diet alongside IF don't want sugar and carbs in their food.

Use tahini on a sandwich, dip, or toss it into a smoothie. You can even eat it by the spoonful to gently break your fast.

Tahini contains loads of healthy fats, protein, and lots of calcium, iron, and B vitamins.

**Frozen Zucchini and/or Peas**

I bet you didn't know that you could use frozen zucchini or peas in place of frozen bananas or other fruits? They literally taste the same when mixed into a smoothie. Sometimes, you don't want all the sugar that is in a banana, so using zucchini instead will help you out.

Zucchini and peas are both extremely nutrient dense.

**Avocado**

Avocado is a wonderful way to get healthy fats back into your diet if they are lacking. You can use mashed or pureed avocado in place of mayonnaise!

Pureed avocado can be used on sandwiches, as dip, or even as a creamy base in different recipes.

## Dark Chocolate

Are you craving sugary chocolate milk but don't want all the carbs? Have a piece of dark chocolate, instead. This little power house of yumminess is actually quite high in nutrients.

Dark chocolate contains a ton of antioxidants. You can swap it instead of eating milk chocolate.

## Ground Flax Seeds

A great swap for wheat germ is ground flax seeds. Add a little to your yogurt, kefir, rice, or ice cream for added nutrition.

Falx seeds are full of fiber, healthy fats, and protein.

## Dark leafy Greens

Did you know that iceberg lettuce is pretty much all water? It isn't bad for you, but it isn't necessarily good for you either as it lacks in nutrients. You can enjoy a more nutritious salad by swapping the iceberg lettuce for dark, leafy greens.

Dark leafy greens are high in vitamins K, E, A, C, and B.

## Cooked Oatmeal and/or Quinoa

Swapping our cold cereal for cooked oats and quinoa is always a good idea. For starters, most commercially made cold cereal is nothing but a big old bag of sugar.

Use oats and quinoa in porridges, hot cereal, and even baked goods.

Oats and quinoa are loaded with fiber, protein, and don't contain any added sugars.

**Coconut Milk**

If you are looking for a more natural milk that contains a ton of healthy fats and medium chain triglycerides, consider swapping out your cow's milk for coconut. Plus, you won't find any harmful chemicals, hormones, or steroids in coconut milk.

Use coconut milk in place of dairy milk in smoothies, soups, sauces, gravies, and to make heavy whipping cream.

**5:2 Fasting – Low Calorie Day Foods**

I wanted to make sure you have a clear idea of what 500 – 600 calories look like, if you're going with the 5:2 method. You may not think that it is a lot of food, but truthfully, it is!

A normally lunch or breakfast for the healthy eater is usually right around 600 – 800 calories.

To help prepare you, I've created a list of foods that fall into the 500-600 calories bracket. As you are starting out on this IF method, you can choose from this list as a beginning point when thinking about the foods you'll be eating on your fasting days. In time, you'll be able to eyeball a 500-calorie meal.

- A plateful of raw or cooked vegetables
- A bowl of Greek yogurt sweetened by a tablespoon of honey and a handful of berries
- Several eggs prepared any way you like them with a strip of bacon
- 3 ounces of grilled fish or meat
- A bowl of riced cauliflower with a tablespoon of pesto
- A large bowl of soup with half of an egg salad sandwich
- Frozen meals that do not exceed 500-600 calories
- 2 veggie burgers with 1 tbsp of mustard

This is a list of enough low-calorie foods to get you through an entire month of 5:2 fasting. Make sure you are drinking plenty of non-calorie fluids on fasting days.

## Pick Fasting Times That Are Right for You

This is very important to ensuring your success on an intermittent fasting diet. You want to pick a timeframe that works best for you. If you work a third shift job, for example, you may not want your eating window to fall during the daytime hours because you'll be asleep.

Are you a breakfast lover? Don't choose fasting times that run into breakfast. You want fasting to work for you, and it doesn't have to be miserable.

Do you have any special events coming up in the near future? Take these events into consideration and modify your fasts around them. Nobody wants to be stuck fasting on their wedding day.

## Stay Busy

Did you know that one of the best ways you can keep yourself from being hungry is by staying busy? When you distract yourself with other activities, you won't find yourself sitting around and lusting over food.

Here are a few ideas on how you can keep your mind off of hunger:

- Read a book
- Journal
- Go for a bike ride
- Walk on a hiking trail
- Go for a swim
- Take a dance class

- Yoga
- Deep clean your house
- Visit your local library
- Go shopping for new clothes (you'll need them because of all the weight you will lose)
- Paint a picture
- Write a poem
- Work in your yard/garden
- Do a fun activity with your kids
- Take your dog for a walk
- Rearrange your kitchen cupboards
- Clean your car
- Go visit a friend
- Do something nice for your neighbor

This list could literally go on for days. Use your imagination and engage in activities that are healthy and productive.

**Start Writing**

You've heard me mention journaling multiple times in this book. Even if you don't view yourself a writer, that's okay, you can still journal. Writing down your feelings, thoughts, and goals about intermittent fasting can be quite therapeutic. Sometimes, when we can see our struggles down on paper, it puts the real issue into perspective.

Make a list of pros and cons about your current eating situation and how you want to improve your health through IF. Don't forget to write down your goals and to celebrate when you meet them.

Journaling is good for the soul. A lot of people who journal during a weight loss program find that they meet their goals easier than folks who do not.

## Remove Negative People from Your Life

Do you have friends and family that don't support your IF lifestyle? Are there just some people in your life that don't "get it"? Ditch them.

Okay, so you can't get rid of your family, but you can choose to not let their comments bother you.

Friends and acquaintances that are non-supportive can easily be put on mute. I'm not saying you have to forget about them but try to avoid bringing up IF when you're around them. There is no sense in talking about something that is important to you when they refuse to understand the science behind fasting.

There are going to be some people out there that think you're starving yourself. They are going to strongly believe that we need three meals a day with snacks in order to be healthy. That is their choice.

However, you have a choice, too. Don't allow their opinions to sabotage your goals.

## Basic Summary of an Intermittent Fasting Schedule

- If you are training, eat for 8 hours of the day and fast for the remaining 16
- On the days your do cardio, eat 9 hours of the day and fast for 15
- Weight lift at least 3 days per week
- Perform cardo at least 2 to 4 times per week
- When you are weight training, maintain your muscle by adding 500 extra calories to your plate
- Only consume carbs on your weight lifting days

Now, this schedule isn't for everyone, obviously. However, if you are an athlete or into bodybuilding, you might find it helpful as you get started on your weight lifting journey.

Feel free to make modifications as you see fit. This is only an example. You may wish to only fast one 24-hour period during your times of training and that is fine. Test out what works best for you.

The above plan is a fat-loss specific program and will help pave the way for bulking up.

Let's get into a bit more detail about the above plan and learn why we would follow such a program to lose fat, shall we?

When you are fasting on weight lifting days, you want there to be an even balance of fasting and eating. You fast will be broken by a pre-workout protein smoothie. Make sure you consume this smoothie at least 15 to 30 minutes before doing your workout. Then, you'll fast for 8 hours.

When doing cardio, you'll break your fast an hour after your last workout and then fast again for 9 hours.

Now, as someone who is trying to lose pure body fat and pave the way for building muscle, you will want to pay attention to your macronutrients. This means you need to determine how many carbs, proteins, fats, and calories you need to be consuming. These figures are based off things like your BMI, height, and weight. It'll take a special math formula to figure out. If you want, you can search macronutrient calculators on the internet and simply plug your information in. You'll have your MACROS in no time flat.

Calories for weight loss depend on whether it is an off-training day or on. It also depends on whether you are lifting weights or doing cardio.

To figure this all out you must first determine the number of calories needed for maintaining your fat loss. The simplest way to do this is to multiply your weight in pounds by fifteen.

Keep in mind, as you lose weight, your macronutrients will change so you'll have to adjust them accordingly. I suggest making tweaks every 2 weeks, especially if you are training.

Now, let's take a look at the macronutrient breakdown on weight lifting days.

- **Fat**

You don't want to exceed 30 grams of fat per day. It truly doesn't matter where the fat comes from as long as it is not from hydrogenated or partially hydrogenated sources. Those types of fat are extremely inflammatory.

- **Protein**

In order to determine the amount of protein you'll need per day, simply multiply your weight by 1.25. So, if you are 200 pounds you will need a minimum of 250 grams of protein per day to preserve your muscle mass. It really doesn't matter where you get your protein from. You can eat bacon if you want, too. Try to add a variety of protein sources into your diet like chicken, beef, and cheese. If you enjoy protein shakes, have them.

- **Carbs**

Carbs should be eaten sparingly as they turn to sugar in your blood stream. Now, weight lifters need more carbs than non-lifters because carbs replenish fuel in the muscles. However, you should not go over 30 grams of carbs in any given day. You want to keep carb intake below 100 grams.

## Make Sure You Are Being Safe

Intermittent fasting is all about improving your health, reducing the risk of sicknesses, and promoting long life. If all of these things are what brought you to intermittent fasting in the first place, please go about doing it, safely. It makes no sense trying to improve your health with intermittent fasting and going about it the wrong way. All you'll end up doing is hurting yourself rather than helping yourself. This would defeat the purpose of your health goals.

## Having Cheat Days

There is a lot of controversy over whether you should have cheat days while intermittent fasting or not. Personally, I do not engage in cheat days because I feel like I get a "cheat" every time I refeed. I always make sure to have a small dessert with my dinner. To me, cheat days do not make any sense while living an intermittent fasting lifestyle.

However, who am I to judge? What works for me may not be the ticket for others. So, I'll explain to you a few reasons why other people claim cheat days are a good thing. You can determine if they are for you or not.

So, basically, some folks feel cheat days are necessary for faster weight loss. The theory behind this concept is that you need to shock your system so that it doesn't get used to fasting and stop causing you to lose weight.

What you would do is start off by eating a ton of junk foods that are high in carbs for one entire day. Go ahead and have the pizza, cake, cookies, and beer. Eat. It. All.

The next day, you are going to keep your calories extremely low. Because you ate so much the previous day, it is thought that your body is ripe for weight loss if you restrict your calories on this day.

You should not take in more than 500 calories and you should exercise to maximize the results.

On day 3, you should eat very low calories but more than you did the day before. Most people see results on the scale by only consuming 1000 calories.

You'll want to give your body a little pop of fuel with some carbohydrates on day 4. Try following a 40% carb, 30% protein, and 30% fat program, today.

On day 5 you will consume nothing but protein. You want to deplete your glucose stores to keep your body wondering what on earth is going on. Why? Because you have another cheat day on the horizon.

Repeat this cycle for an entire month and see what your results are and how you feel. If it is a good way for you to fast, stick with it. If not, kick it to the curb.

**Elderly People and IF**

When you think of people of advanced age, you probably picture sickly, frail folks who are bedridden or in nursing homes. Why do we have this image in our minds? Because it is what we see. For most, elderly people are sick, and some are even overweight.

Intermittent fasting is not a concept those of the senior citizen community widely accept. They have been taught that you "clean your plate" and you don't skip meals, for health purposes. Many folks of the senior citizen community are also Depression Era survivors, and during that time, you did not waste food because it was uncertain whether you'd be eating any time soon again or not.

This constant cycle of eating has broken down their bodies and plunged them right into the aging process. Imagine if your grandparents had been on a fasting schedule their entire lives?

They might look and feel better today. Perhaps, some of their age-related illnesses wouldn't exist in their lives.

Elderly folks can certainly participate in an intermittent fasting schedule. However, it needs to be modified to fit their needs. Their doctor should also be made aware of their plans. Older people should not be fasting for 24-hours though and they should not be engaged in rigorous exercise. Light exercise coupled with a few 16:8 fast days might be ideal for the mature adult.

There are some doctors who actually support short-term fasting for the elderly and recommend it for a variety of their patients. Some docs have claimed that fasting helps relieve the symptoms pf Parkinson's and Alzheimer's Disease.

If you are a senior citizen and would like to give intermittent fasting a try, please discuss it over with your doctor before getting started.

**Give IF a Solid Month**

If after the first few days on IF you feel discouraged and want to throw in the towel, don't do it. Your body is getting used to a very new way of eating. It needs time to undo years of patterns and schedules. This isn't going to happen overnight.

Tell yourself that you are committing to a solid 30 days of intermittent fasting. If at the end of the 30 days, you still feel that the IF lifestyle isn't something you can handle, that's okay. At least you didn't give up before you even got started.

# Fasting Resources

Here is a list of various websites that you can turn to for fasting helping and guidance.

500 calories meal ideas

https://www.womanmagazine.co.uk/diet-food/500-calorie-meal-plans-52-diet-29560

Dr. Jason Fung

https://www.dietdoctor.com/authors/dr-jason-fung-m-d

IDM Program

https://idmprogram.com/

Dr. Eric Berg

https://www.drberg.com/

Dr. Eric Berg YouTube Channel

https://www.youtube.com/channel/UC3w193M5tYPJqF0Hi-7U-2g

The Warrior Diet

https://www.healthline.com/nutrition/warrior-diet-guide

5:2 Method

https://the5-2dietbook.com/basics

16:8 Method

https://www.healthline.com/nutrition/16-8-intermittent-fasting

Alternate Day Fasting

https://www.healthline.com/nutrition/alternate-day-fasting-guide

OMAD

https://omaddiet.com/

Eat-Stop-Eat

https://www.livestrong.com/article/438695-how-eat-stop-eat-works/

Dr. Josh Axe

https://draxe.com/

Specific IF Links

https://blog.bulletproof.com/intermittent-fasting-guide/

https://dailyburn.com/life/health/intermittent-fasting-methods/

https://qz.com/1419105/a-diet-guru-explains-why-you-should-eat-dinner-at-2pm/

https://www.scientificamerican.com/article/how-intermittent-fasting-might-help-you-live-longer-healthier-life/

# CONCLUSION

Intermittent fasting is something that should be approached with positivity. You want to know and understand the process before you hop on board. Hopefully, this book has made the science behind IF a little clearer for you.

When I first started my intermittent fasting journey, I didn't really know what I was doing. I just hopped right in. As I got deeper into IF, I realized I needed to educate myself on what I was doing to my body. I am so glad that I did!

Any weight loss program is going to be easier when you understand its basic principles. Unlike other health and wellness eating programs, intermittent fasting is seriously simple. There are no calories to count, no special foods, and no exercise routines. You eat and then you don't it.

That's how you make intermittent fasting work for you. You keep it simple. I encourage you to try out the 30-day fasting guide that is enclosed in this book and choose the best way to IF for you.

Don't be afraid to ask questions! There are a ton of Facebook groups that are all about intermittent fasting. Join a few of these groups and talk with others who are on the same path that you are. Having a strong support system is imperative.

I hope you enjoyed this book and where able to glean all sorts of IF gems from its pages. Know that your journey won't always be easy, but you are strong, capable, and able to meet your goals.

I believe in you!

28325276R00075

Made in the USA
Lexington, KY
13 January 2019